POETRY 2000

The Poet Within the Poet

O I am Virgil, Milton, Keats,
I wear their language, their conceits,
Within their shadows, page by page,
I read their sadness or their rage.
I think their thoughts of arms I sing,
Of Edens vanished with the spring,
Of autumn fruit that seemed divine;
I speak dead words and call them mine.

But is there in this glib pretence
Of rhyming, scanning, making sense
A second self you do not see
Clothed in a warmer poetry?
A self regretting wasted years
Spent weeping other people's tears,
That takes its secret, evening stroll
In the private summers of the soul?

And wishes, when that soul is bared,
It had an audience that cared.

by Frank McDonald

POETRY 2000

Poems from the Literary Review

Edited by Clarissa Burden
Introduced by Auberon Waugh

Robson Books

First published in Great Britain in 2000 by Robson Books,
10 Blenheim Court, Brewery Road, London N7 9NT

A member of the Chrysalis Group plc

Copyright © 2000 Literary Review

The right of Clarissa Burden to be identified as the author of this work has been asserted by her in accordance with the Copyright, Designs and Patents Act 1988

British Library Cataloguing in Publication Data
A catalogue record for this title is available from the British Library

ISBN 1 86105 380 0

All rights reserved. No part of this publication may be reproduced, stored in a retrieval system, or transmitted in any form or by any means, electronic, mechanical, photocopying, recording or otherwise, without the prior permission in writing of the publishers.

Printed in Great Britain by Creative Print & Design (Wales), Ebbw Vale

Contents

Introduction by Auberon Waugh ... ix
Editor's Note ... xi

September 1996 – WILD LIFE
D A Prince ... 1
Paul Griffin ... 3
Giles de la Bédoyère ... 4

October 1996 – SEWERS
Noel Petty ... 6
Francis Mullen ... 7

November 1996 – TREASON
Griselda Scott ... 9
Alison Prince ... 11
D Shepherd ... 12

December 1996 – OUR GLORIOUS BRITISH PRESS
C B Owen ... 13
Noel Petty ... 14
Stephen Constable ... 15
Jane Edmond ... 16

January 1997 – JOYS OF TRAVEL
Richard Charles ... 17
Christine Whittemore ... 18

February 1997 – THE STALKER
David Poole ... 19
Philip A Nicholson ... 20
D A Prince ... 21
Alison Mortimer ... 22

March 1997 – WESTERING HOME
John Lord ... 23
Griselda Scott ... 24
Brian Mitchell ... 25
Philip A Nicholson ... 26

April 1997 – FIN DE SIÈCLE
Frank McDonald ... 27
J M Harvey ... 28
Barbara Daniels ... 29
Bill Greenwell ... 30

May 1997 – SUGAR DADDY
Richard Charles ... 31
Philip A Nicholson ... 32
Isabel Vincent ... 33
Paul Griffin ... 34

June 1997 – DIANA RE-CLOTHED
Frank McDonald ... 35

July 1997 – SANDWICHES
Brian Mitchell ... 36
Griselda Scott ... 37

August 1997 – FIGS
Alison Prince 38
Mick Humphreys 39
Alanna Blake 40
Fiona Pitt-Kethley 41
Jane Falloon 42

September 1997 – WATER
Laurence Joyce 43
Fergus Gwynplaine
 MacIntyre 45
Robert Jules Vincent 46

October 1997 – HUNTING
Vincent L Smith 47
Barbara Daniels 48
D Shepherd 49
Prue Sheldon 50

November 1997 – FRAILTY
Norman Bissett 51
Isabel Vincent 52

December 1997 – BLISS
O Smith 53
Angela Greenhill 54
Rannoch Melville Russell 55

January 1998 – TWO FACES
Robert Jules Vincent 56
Fiona Pitt-Kethley 57
Jenny Proom 58

February 1998 – CHILDREN FROM HELL
Noel Petty 59
M Hammerton 60
Richard Charles 61

March 1998 – IN PRAISE OF PLUMPNESS
Philip A Nicholson 62
D A Prince 63
John Kerkhoven 64
O Smith 65
Noel Petty 66

April 1998 – FROLIC
Joan Butler 67
D Shepherd 68
Katie Mallett 69
John Wedge 70

May 1998 – FISH
O Smith 71
Alison Prince 72
John Lord 73
Mary Holtby 74

June 1998 – KITH AND KIN
Richard Charles 75
Laurence Joyce 76

July 1998 – QUIETNESS
Richard Charles 77
Noel Petty 78
Caspian Richards 79
Pamela Martin 80

August 1998 – CHOIRBOYS	
Richard Charles	81
O Smith	82
Paul Griffin	83
Maureen A Jeffs	84
September 1998 – PASSION	
Jonathan Pool	85
J M Harvey	86
Terence Reid	87
David Rogers	88
October 1998 – MY HEART LEAPS UP	
Noel Petty	89
Ted Giles	90
Philip A Nicholson	91
November 1998 – LUNCH	
Jon Sayers	92
Joan Butler	94
Alanna Blake	96
December 1998 – BUILDING	
Richard Charles	97
D A Prince	98
D Shepherd	99
Mick Humphreys	100
January 1999 – REQUITED LOVE	
Martin Piper	101
Noel Petty	102
Frank McDonald	103
Alison Prince	104

February 1999 – MEMORY LOSS	
Richard Charles	105
Ted Giles	106
D Shepherd	107
Frank McDonald	108
March 1999 – CACOPHONY	
Ralph Rochester	109
Alfred Peter Hollick	110
D Shepherd	111
April 1999 – SPRING CLEANING	
Laurence Joyce	112
Diana Newlands	113
Andrew Brison	114
Richard Otto	115
Angela Greenhill	116
May 1999 – TRESPASS	
Ralph Rochester	117
Adèle Geras	118
June 1999 – A CURIOUS HOBBY	
Noel Petty	119
Richard Charles	120
Maureen A Jeffs	121
July 1999 – HARMONY	
Alison Prince	122
Bill Philips	123
Mick Humphreys	124

August 1999 – SUMMER FOLLIES
Angela Greenhill 125
Frank McDonald 126
David Hill 127
Maureen A Jeffs 128

September 1999 – LIPS THAT LIE
Jack Carrigan 129
Nick Syrett 130
Patricia V Dawson 131

October 1999 – PSALM
O Smith 132
Joan Butler 133

November 1999 – THE FALL
Alison Prince 134
Frank McDonald 135
Katie Mallett 136

December 1999/January 2000 – DALLIANCE
Noel Petty 137
J M Harvey 138
Frank McDonald 139
Philip A Nicholson 140

February 2000 – IN PRAISE OF SLOUGH
J M Turner 141
Robert Marks 142
Angela Greenhill 143

March 2000 – MONEY
Noel Petty 144
Janice Novaya 145
Ted Giles 146

April 2000 – WEDNESDAY
Paul Griffin 147
Colonel G H Peebles 148
Maureen Brampton 149

May 2000 – LAST LOVE
Richard Charles 150
Catherine Dampier 151
Derek Muncey 152

July 2000 – LONDON
D A Prince 153
Edward Murch 154
Iain Colley 155
Colin Pearson 156

July 2000 – FOREIGN PARTS
Robert Marks 157
Alanna Blake 158
W H Jarvis 159
D E Poole 160

Index of Poems 161

Introduction
by Auberon Waugh

The fourth anthology of *Literary Review*'s poems which rhyme and scan, addressed to a set subject, appears at a promising moment. Perhaps the arrival of Andrew Motion as Poet Laureate helped convince people that the modern movement has finally run out of steam. Public patronage is still in the control of the various academic establishments, rewarding any sort of prosaic drivel. But public indifference is slowly – very slowly – turning into resentment. The educated classes no longer see opacity as flattering to their intelligence, but as insulting to their common sense. Above all, there is an awareness that poems which neither rhyme, nor scan, nor make sense, are boring to read.

Introducing the second volume, *A Burning Candle* (Poetry Now 1993) I reported on the hostility which had greeted the first in places like Birmingham. They said they thought it old-fashioned and out-moded, but I think their resentment derived from the suggestion of what is nowadays called élitism – the reminder of an older, richer culture that their own.

Be that as it may, one observes that middlebrow and popular newspapers are now printing the occasional poem which rhymes and scans, more often than not sent in by a reader. Perhaps it is a sign of intellectual insecurity in newspapers like the *Guardian*, *Observer* and *TLS* that they continue to give space to the old rubbish, always on the insistence of their poetry editors, who are modernists to a man and woman.

In time, no doubt, they will realise they are making fools of themselves and sack the poetry editors. There will always be Labour councils happy to employ them in one capacity or another. I think they have been running scared for quite a long time. It may be significant that although very few anthologies of new poetry are published, the first three volumes of this series (all, alas, completely sold out and unprocurable) never received a single review.

If poetry editors had had the necessary confidence in their cause, they could have torn the enterprise to shreds. Each volume contains a hundred-odd poems chosen from the 500-odd printed in the period. They are reckoned to be the better poems, but by no means all of them are very good and some are quite bad. Many have duff lines. By concentrating on bad poems and duff lines, they could have presented the whole idea of formal poetry as an absurdity and disaster in this day and age. Instead, they chose to ignore it.

After 14 years of effort at *Literary Review*, it begins to look as if formal poetry is coming back in the popular imagination. The twelve or so members of our poetry panel, who meet unpaid and unacknowledged to judge the 120-odd poems which arrive every month, will be gratified, but we have no serious claim to have brought it about. Above all, we would not wish to discourage any other newspaper or magazine from running a similar or identical competition. With this edition, Clarissa Burden takes over from Dariane Pictet as editor, both of who must be thanked profusely for their selfless, unrewarded work. The truth is that the whole enterprise, like the *Literary Review* itself, runs on nothing but good will. It is most encouraging to learn that there is so much of it around.

Editor's Note

'Poetry,' Saint Augustine is alleged to have said, 'is the wine of the devil.' In order to emphasise its more enjoyable aspects, *Poetry 2000* offers one hundred and fifty-three of the best short, lyric poems, entered for the famous *Literary Review* monthly competition over the past four years.

Some of the subjects set have been high-flown: Requited Love, Dalliance and Lips that Lie, safe inspiration for a poet's coy muse; others were more commonplace, for instance Sewers and Money. But the response of the poets to these diverse topics has always been generous and imaginative. Some very unlikely subjects produced excellent results: Choirboys, Figs, In Praise of Plumpness and, strangely enough, Spring Cleaning – all brought in resourceful entries of a very high standard. Subjects which make them laugh are always popular with the judges, but the more serious and thoughtful poems are well represented here. There is no way to predict whether a subject will inspire poets to excellence or whether it will produce sloppy or lazy results. Abstract ideas such as Harmony and Bliss have attracted the same number of entries as the more mundane like London and In Praise of Slough. Indeed, it has seemed at times that the more refractory the subject set, for example Wednesday or Sandwiches, the deeper the poets have plunged into their creative psyche. Whatever the topic required, the varied and often surprising interpretations contribute hugely to the enjoyment of these poems.

Above all, it is the poets, many of whom send in admirable contributions month after month, who deserve congratulations and gratitude for their determination to hold the traditional banner of lyric poetry courageously and defiantly aloft.

Clarissa Burden

Wild Life

WILD LIFE

"This Area is Reserved for the Wildlife"
(Notice in St James's Park)

Wildlife cringing in the dark
Jungle called St James's Park,
What official hand decreed
Private places where you feed?

Why, with wat'ry depths around
Must you lurk in hidden ground?
Do the tourists make you blench?
Earnest Germans, friv'lous French?

Pochard, pintail, mallard, duck,
Can you not believe your luck?
On St James's grassy meads
What committee plots your needs?

What the pencil? what the pen?
What the mind that banished men?
Whose voice authorised this board
That keeps out the tourist hoard?

When the mammoth roamed the earth
And the dinosaur gave birth
Did they smirk when fences banned
Hunter/gatherers from their land?

WILD LIFE

Pelican and squirrel, do
You require this haven too?
Do you tremble at the knees
Faced with ranks of Japanese?

Wildlife, wildlife, looking tame,
Lumped together by this name,
Who's the watchdog keeps you here
In St James's urban sphere?

Wildlife, looking less than wild,
Less like tiger, more like child,
Less like savage, more like meek:
Are you really what we seek?

by D A Prince

Wild Life

When I shall die, it will be overeating
Or over-something else that lays me flat;
My cause of death: "Wild Life". That takes some beating.
What's "General Decrepitude" to that?
What's "Atrophy", and all those other phrases,
The careful half-truths practised by the quacks,
With which they send us underneath the daisies,
Replace their fountain pens, and turn their backs?
When I shall die, I shall be full to bursting
And living passionate enraptured nights,
Intent upon the joys I am immersed in,
Singing with pleasure, on the very heights.
I lie, of course: I'll quietly . . . not be here.
"Oh, him?" you'll say; "I thought he died last year."

by Paul Griffin

Game

Too old to chase a quarry on the hoof,
She fed off human victims whom she found:
And, though remaining cannily aloof,
Left grisly relics strewn across the ground.

The tigress, whose career seemed near its end
Since age had almost worn her teeth away,
Employed her weight to fell, her claws to rend,
But used her full-grown cub to kill the prey.

Week after week, a famous hunter stalked
This man-eating marauder and her son;
Wherever wound the tracks his footsteps walked,
He searched in vain for traces: there were none.

A slaughtered cow, descried from wooded heights,
Awarded him a single lucky break.
He got the feasting couple in his sights -
Then found he'd shot the youngster by mistake.

Outwitted, stumped, acknowledging defeat,
He started homeward, reaching a ravine
With narrow walls impeding his retreat,
Not knowing that, unseeing, he was seen . . .

Taut instinct sensed, before he saw, the foe
Poised on a rock-ledge, perilously near.
The arm which raised his gun moved deadly-slow,
Disguising his intent – and sudden fear.

Aware of having won their duel, while
Anxious to hasten slow starvation's death,
She smiled (he swore) a last triumphant smile
And only then gave up her final breath.

Those who pursue striped majesty for sport,
A blazoned rug or proudly mounted head,
Might spare one sober, self-demeaning thought:
The beast may be exploiting them, instead.

by Giles de la Bédoyère

Sewers

The Undercurrent

The sewers are crumbling: under the streets
Those hardly-imagined Victorian feats
Of engineer's vision and Irishman's spade
A century on, are cracked and decayed.
Beneath all the traffic and grinding of gears,
The sewers are crumbling, and nobody hears.

In the hospital ward, many floors above ground,
The lordly consultant proceeds on his round.
The surgeon trades organs, and cuts without knives,
While freezers store ready-made small human lives.
But down in the darkness the fissuring breeds;
The sewers are crumbling, and nobody heeds.

From the city's wired palaces, shining and high,
Electronic fortunes are bounced off the sky;
When you're playing the brave post-industrial game
Information is all: physicality's tame.
But down in the earth physicality grows;
The sewers are crumbling, and nobody knows.

A sewer, it's true, has little appeal
Compared to a cordon bleu restaurant meal,
Two cars in the drive, or a week on the Med –
The cradle of civilisation, it's said –
But here there's another one, needing repair;
The sewers are crumbling, and nobody's there.

by Noel Petty

Home is where the Shit is

The stench is sickening. The others say
I'll soon get used to it. I hope that's right.
I used to sleep in doorways, with some hay
By way of pillow. Then, one dreadful night,
Men with guns came, off-duty policemen. They
Killed everybody else. I'd taken flight.
Clearly, the time had come to disappear.
I stole a torch and found my way down here.

There are five others: Jaime, who's half blind,
Dolores, who keeps saying she's unwell,
Pablo, who thinks we mustn't be unkind,
At least to one another, Isabel,
Who never speaks, and Ana, who's resigned
To giving birth – at NINE! – oh, bloody hell:
What kind of world is this? I'll kill the sod
Who did this to her. Where the devil's God?

WE are the sewage, voided for the good
Of the community. No one wants to know
About us; no one sees that we have food,
Clothing and shelter. Lowest of the low,
We thieve by day: at night, we talk, or brood
Until we sleep. Some day a vast inflow
Of rainwater will drown us all, and we
Will end up in the all-embracing sea.

SEWERS

Some talk of a redeemer, who descends
Into our depths, and liberates from hell
The likes of us, cloacal Christ, who bends
To bless and nourish. Bollocks! You can tell
That one to the Marines. I and my friends
Will go on being loathsome things that smell,
(I speak of tragedy in terms of farce)
Six little turds dropped from Society's arse.

by Francis Mullen

Treason

Love's Treachery

She listens now with disobedient mind
To words that gave her rapture in her youth
From such a man. In days when love was blind
His every word stood for her as the truth.

And still she kneels beside him at his prayers
With thought adrift but anxious not to break
The valued link he still assumes as theirs.
She holds her kindly silence for his sake.

On Sundays, sitting in her lonely pew,
An upward smile as he begins to preach
She fondly gives. That is at least his due
For powerful words that many hearts will reach.

Should she have told him they no longer met
Her need; that reasoning had led her out
Of narrow confines? She could not as yet
Devise a gentle way to own to doubt.

It would be torture to him that her soul
Was facing danger, all his teaching vain
Now he and she no longer shared the goal
Of Heaven; on death, would never meet again.

All questioning is sacrilege to him,
His loving God reserving punishment
For those who leave the Faith to follow whim,
Misled by Satan's specious argument.

TREASON

As she imagines him among the Blessed,
She feels for him the hurt of his surprise
At learning, her confession not addressed,
That love had, by its silence, dealt in lies.

by Griselda Scott

The Traitor

"I heard her laugh," he said. "That's when I knew."
He stared out at the cedar-shadowed lawn.
"It was the year our granddaughter was born.
I told myself at first it wasn't true -
I'd known the Kirby-Smiths for twenty years,
Betty and Tom. Then Betty died, of course.
Breast cancer. Poor old Tom, he felt the loss
So badly. One night he broke down in tears
At dinner. Damned embarrassing. And Clare
Reached out and put her hand on his, so calm
And comforting, my lovely wife. Her arm
Was very white. Sweet peas scented the air
And red wine gravy. Pheasant. Funny how
These things come back." He paused. "I didn't mind,
You know. I wasn't jealous. She was always kind,
I liked that. But of course, I wonder now
How long the pair of them – drink up." He poured
Another stiffish whisky. "I suppose
I was a rather dull man. Goodness knows
I tried to keep her happy. She was bored,
Though, I can see that. But I never meant
To overhear them down there by the pool.
Her throaty laugh . . . God, I was such a fool."
He shrugged. "And three days after that, she went."
I felt for him. Such things must leave a scar.
"And bloody Tom," he said, "borrowed my car."

by Alison Prince

Brutus

I have with honour served the Roman State,
Borne arms, held office, as a Roman should,
And often in the Senate have I stood
And spoken with conviction in debate
Opposing strongly advocates of change.
Caesar of course I knew: beyond compare
As statesman, soldier, leader; well aware
Of what ambition might with skill arrange.

He wanted monarchy, the Roman crown.
Anathema to me – and others too.
There was no choice in what we had to do
With such a man: he had to be cut down.
We knew that it was treason, that our shrouds
Were ready if our schemes should go astray
But Rome was at our feet for one whole day
'Til that fool Antony stirred up the crowds.

Now is the end. We've come to our account
For this is Philippi and all is lost,
Nothing accomplished at enormous cost
And sly Octavian left paramount.
By me a second treason must be tried
Wherein the victim's by himself betrayed
And all the debts he has incurred are paid
Once and for all. This treason's suicide.

by D Shepherd

Our Glorious British Press

Sleet Street

The satyr of mythology
Had curious, cloven feet,
However thick the mud it kicked
Its coat stayed clean and neat.
He may surpass the satyr
Who learns the scribbler's trade,
A column inch will, at a pinch,
Outspatter hoof or spade,
Nor will he miss that pittance
His lawyers term redress
Who wins each day what people pay
To see the greater less.

by C B Owen

Feeding of the Terrier

The British Pressbull stands foursquare
For Freedom, Truth and Playing Fair.
Fresh blood-red meat is all he asks
To carry out these noble tasks.
In short, the British Pressbull is
The fountain of our liberties.

Unlike the Gallic poodle breed
That does exactly as decreed,
Or German *hund* that never howls
And thinks three times before it growls,
The British Pressbull roams at will,
A privateer, licensed to kill.

One hint of anything unclean
Will bring him bounding to the scene,
And if some random passer-by
Should lose a finger or an eye,
Why, that's no reason for alarm –
The good he does outweighs the harm.

Raw meat will keep him in the pink,
As well as lots and lots to drink.
Fresh air, too – though he tends to pick
The wrong end, if you throw a stick,
And guards the right to drop his poos
On any doorstep he might choose.

If all this sounds like too much strife,
Remember this: *A dog's for life.*
And though sometimes you're bound to think
You'd like a bit less noise and stink,
I can't believe that you'd allow
Him to be fettered; would you, now?

by Noel Petty

Mirrors and Windows

But each may *choose* his window; stare
So sly, or shameless, at the pass
Of crooks and kingdoms, while aware
How cracked, distorted, is the glass
By mere man made, for him to view
Man's greater imperfections. Pain,
Loss, passion, hate, despair, seen through
His own breath's mist upon the pane.

And each may choose his mirror. How
He sees himself, he sees mankind;
What revelations hold him now
Reflect his taste, his creed, his mind,
His aspirations – wealth, power, lust,
Renown or infamy. The whole
Or partial image he can trust
To show not just his face, but soul.

by Stephen Constable

Two Faced

Our great and glorious British press
Provides, from Cornwall to Caithness,
Its readers with the sober face
Of news about the human race
And politics here and abroad.
Informed thus daily, we applaud:
The well-considered text and views
This press responsibly pursues;
Its fearless journalistic sleuths
Who ferret out important truths;
And fair, objective but robust
Reporting one can mostly trust.

Our mean and grubby British press,
Intrusive, brash, slow to redress
Mistakes, half-truths and downright lies,
Prefers to print and dramatise
Life's vulgar and salacious news,
(The bits and tits we plebs peruse!)
Gleaned slyly by long distance lens
And rat-packs with capricious pens!
The cheque books, flashed around as well,
Lure grasping hands; and "kiss-and-tell"
Discarded lovers – any age -
Get splashed across the whole front page!

But all the pages, mean and clean,
End up together, going green,
Stuffed chastely in recycling skips -
Or wrapped around hot fish and chips!

by Jane Edmond

Joys of Travel

Das Brandopfer

We travelled for ages, a twenty-hour drive,
Packed shoulder to rib, nose to tail.
They put us in cages to keep us alive,
So our meat wasn't frozen or stale.

We went to the seaside to sail off to sea.
Policemen were lining the street.
Heroes fought on the quayside that we might be free,
And saints threw themselves at our feet.

In our millions we burned when they said we were mad
And all of our kind had to die;
And nobody turned up, and no-one was sad,
And nobody bothered to cry.

by Richard Charles

JOYS OF TRAVEL

A Journey

We took a journey down the roads near Rome,
sailing a borrowed car from town to town;
no press of time, no hurry to get home.
I wore a tent-like dress, a hand-me-down,
and, posing for his camera, pulled it tight,
displaying proudly how our child had grown,
feeling my belly ripen like a fruit.

Among the fountains and cascades of Tivoli
we wandered, sometimes stopping to embrace;
the hours to come hung richly, heavily.
Down by the coast, we found the cheapest place
Gaeta had; my interesting state
brought tenderness into the owner's face.
She stopped me at the threshold, made me wait:

I could not enter till I'd tasted food
(though this, I think, ensured her own good luck).
The room she offered qualified as rude,
the doorless doorway low – we had to duck;
the window, with no glass, an open square
cut in the wall. We woke at five o'clock
when dawn blew in, and birds began fanfare.

We set off, groggy, in the morning's cool,
pausing to buy some dewy figs en route.
We reached Sperlonga, stopped by the sea wall,
and there for breakfast ate our bag of fruit.

I've travelled often since, to taste again
the pleasures of that journey: all in vain.
No feast has been as succulent to me
as those fat figs, at sunrise, by the sea.

by Christine Whittemore

The Stalker

The Stalker

Yes, I could take the Frightful Fiend
That close behind me trod:
I turned, then stripped of fear I leaned
Upon the arm of God.

My stalker is no phantom fear
Of opium-shattered mind;
He stops and spreads his hideous leer
From twenty yards behind.

If I approach, one hand he drops
To fiddle with his fly
And with the other quietly strops
His knife upon his tie.

"Come on and take your pick, my dear,
The penis or the knife."
And I must run in abject fear
For sanity or life.

When Satan's clad in human form
God leaves the work to men
Who say to me: "He can't perform.
Don't fret about old Ben.

We wouldn't let him bother you
Unless we were quite sure
He's on the mend; a credit to
The latest Social Cure."

THE STALKER

So I must sleep in fits at night
- Or wake with sickening lurch
To hear beneath a shuddering light:
"The cure needs more research;

We thank you for your patience, dear;
We're very sorry too
That when he cracked he cracked right here
And took it out on you."

by David Poole

Suicide Note

I cannot shake him off, I've tried,
No tactic ever works,
My sanctuaries are known to him,
Where I hide, he lurks,
Among the peaks of happiness
In the troughs of my despair
In every crevice of my mind
My follower is there,
Yet though he dogs my footsteps
We can never truly meet,
I turn to face him, but to glimpse
His shadowy retreat.
Now I can wait no longer
On the persecutor's whim,
He will not fairly come to me so
I must go to him.

by Philip A Nicholson

Stalking

Too hot an afternoon to hunt: the scent
is all crushed lavender and thyme, and bees
cross-canvassing the catmint. Yet she'll freeze
and flatten, hissing harpoon-clawed intent

for sparrow-weights who scarcely stir the scales.
With needled concentration, belly down,
tail a slow coil of fury, fur a crown
of air-keen senses, she creeps forward; trails

a polished track, grass silvered. Oil-slick quick,
gleaming with expectation, inching through
scorched clover, low on squat piston legs tensed to
the final spring, mouth squaring for the thick

crunch of warmed feathers she's all art. And I,
coward accomplice, do not break her spell,
or make the warning handclap that would tell
her prey to quit the thistle-heads and fly.

by D A Prince

The Stalker

"It will all end in tears," she prophesied,
As we walked together across the sunstreaked lawn.
Her body bent by years, mine at her side
Still straight. "What future is there with someone who's torn
Between two lives? I know . . ." She paused, a touch
Of anger in her now. "Believe me, it is true.
These men with wives," she spat. "They want too much."
She looked at me, grave faced. "It's not the life for you."

But later when she'd gone, I sat and thought
On that: a trug of freshpicked raspberries on the floor.
I hulled them one by one as she had taught
Me once, twisting the stalk and easing out the core,
Careful to place them neatly side by side,
Claret-kissed larvae in a bowl of Chinese white.
Tasting their flesh, sharpsweet, so long denied,
I made the choice to follow the path that was right

For me. The shadows crept into the day
As stalk by stalk I finished off my simple task.
The doubts I'd had were plucked and thrown away
And juice ran ruby from my lips. But never ask
A woman whose soft mouth is stained with red
Just why it is her eyes are bleak. She will dispute
That this life has cost her dear, hope has fled.
No flavour in this world can match forbidden fruit.

by Alison Mortimer

Westering Home

The Dispossessed

For liberty of conscience many sought;
Some, famine-driven, merely hoped for bread;
From poverty or pogrom other fled;
Some had, like beasts, been hunted, sold and bought.
The long Atlantic crossing, danger-fraught,
Unnumbered thousands made, in hope, in dread,
Longing for death, or by bright visions led -
The old world's flotsam to the new world brought.
These, exiles from their home, their kin, their land,
Westward and ever further westward pressed.
No obstacle their purpose could withstand -
From the vast wilderness a home to wrest.
And every fort, farm, cabin saw a band
Of Choctaw, Sioux, Comanche dispossessed.

by John Lord

At Sundowning

Men are ever westward wending
Every birth forebodes its ending
Life gives each its term of lending
Groundling flower to tallest tree.

When the journey's end is nearing
Some give welcome never fearing
Rest to them can seem endearing.
As the day ends so must we.

When the springtime shoots are showing
And the suckling beasts are growing
It is time the old were going -
Death is only living's fee.

by Griselda Scott

Reelin' Hame

Westerin' hame wi' a dracht up yer kilt,
Thinkin' o' times when guid ships were Clyde built,
Aye sure nae drap o' yer malt wad be spilt,
Aa the wa' o'er tae Isla.

Hummin' a tune that ye learnt frae yer Mam
In the auld days o' the cairthorse an' tram,
Helpin' yersel' tae anither wee dram,
Fain tae be bound for Isla.

When ye get there an' ye're still i' the bar,
Ye'll tak a chaser tae counter the haar,
Ony excuse since it's nae verra far
Back tae yer ben in Isla.

by Brian Mitchell

Englishman Abroad

In search of ancient wisdoms, he
Immersed himself in Eastern lore,
Took their country to his heart,
Embraced its customs, life, and art
Became as one of them and saw
Himself as European no more.
But lately in his sleepless hours
Or in the void of idle days
Shades of things he'd left behind
Disturbed his certainty of mind,
The Englishness of Betjeman, cricket on the green,
Cold beds, warm beer, the urban scene,
All that formed and made him
Stoutly British to the bone:
In limbo now he moves between
His present world and what has been
The body disinclined to roam
The soul disposed to wester home.

by Philip A Nicholson

Fin de Siècle

Fin de Siècle

'The old order changeth, yielding place to new.'

Farewell to all tradition gave,
A land of hope, a sceptred isle;
An era ends and in a while
No one will care how sleep the brave.
Where Pippa passes, none shall guess,
And none shall know the winding brook,
And none shall wait with patient look
By Keats's autumn cider-press.
And Pope's Pierian spring will be
Safe from the lips of would-be wise;
Beauty in Byron's starry skies
Shall walk in night, for none to see.

Then who will love you, England, who
Will talk of blue, remembered hills?
Who will be summoned by your bells,
Or note the crags where eagles flew?
Sad how you sink so willingly
Back to the mists from where you rose,
And as the century turns, God knows
What Gray will pen your elegy.

by Frank McDonald

Thé Dansant

The radio plays, late at night, a medley of old tunes
that set dry memories alight, rekindle afternoons
spent sipping tea at the Savoy and drinking in our fill
of sights and sounds – a passing joy but source of pleasure still,

remembering the parquet's gleam; bone china's classy 'chink';
the silver teapot's amber stream and cheeks a trifle pink
from dancing with some debonair, young military man –
all perfect teeth, macassared hair and proud colonial tan –

while hawk-eyed matrons (nodding their approval) ordered buns,
and nimble waiters brushed, with care, the tables free of crumbs;
where Irish linen spread so crisp its spotless formal squares,
and napkins bore the sticky kiss from chocolate éclairs . . .

Now, after long, neglected years, they thought they'd resurrect
the 'tea dance' – polish dull veneers of social etiquette
and bring a little glamour back to bingo afternoons –
a gentle flirt, a tea-time snack, some tasteful, dancing tunes.

But now the orchestra's a tape rewinding on its own,
the music offers no escape – we're in a twilight zone
of formica and lino tiles and paper cups and plates;
denture cream and plastic smiles and Mr Kipling's cakes.

We all remember how to dance but few will take the floor,
we sip our PG Tips and glance unseeing, out the door,
reliving scenes from other times – an era that is gone –
recall the teapot's silver shine; the smell of fresh Souchong.

by J M Harvey

Fin de Siècle

I do not fear the calendar: I know that decades fly,
Time's chariot may catch me up but it dare not pass me by,
I'll race it even faster, though the distance has decreased
And spur on the aging century with an Alexandrian feast.

The guest list is already drawn, I know whom I'll invite,
We'll burn the candle at both ends, yet make it last the night,
We'll drink a draught to decadence, Dionysus unconfined –
Abandon modern pastimes; I have older thrills in mind.

A soupçon of the Gallic should achieve that wicked note:
You can choose your pleasures à la carte or take them table d'hôte,
Chez moi, there'll be what you desire to make your joys complete:
Do you prefer a dash of tonic or do you like your vices neat?

I'll put everything on offer to tempt the bon viveur,
Misrule and impropriety – I declare them de rigueur,
So, if your fancy's tickled, catch my eye across the throng,
And we'll make the Nineties naughty, with élan, on my chaise longue.

by Barbara Daniels

Fin de Siècle

I wallow around in the cold of the ocean,
Or bask by the beaches where foreigners swim:
If I see the leg of a tourist in motion,
I grit all my teeth and make merry with him.

I wish I could copyright all of the fiction
Concocted about me by landlubber bores:
I'd publish rebuttals and flog contradictions –
Or bite all the bastards with both of my jaws.

Instead I cruise carelessly under the waters,
And nibble the limbs of the liar or heckler,
Then swallow, for afters, his sons and his daughters,
Whatever the decade, I'm Fin de Siècle.

by Bill Greenwell

Sugar Daddy

Sweet Talk

I am battered and used, I'm at least second-hand,
And I'm not what I once used to be,
But I've never seen anything like you before.
Can you really be staring at me?

Your limbs and your body are perfect,
And your smile comes as such a surprise,
And you don't look a day over nineteen-years-old,
Except for the fire in your eyes.

Would you sleep with a middle-aged dreamer,
Whose dream turned to ashes and stone,
Who is tired, disillusioned and wrinkled and cold,
And worn out from living alone?

Be my mistress, O be my companion.
Be my mother, my child and my whore.
And I'll be your most faithful admirer,
Your lover, your servant, your lord.

We'll pick up the world by the scruff of its neck,
Shake it senseless and rattle its brains,
And we'll storm through its walls and we'll trample its fields,
And we'll live on ice-cream and champagne.

I'll show you the power of my money,
You can teach me respect and disdain,
And show me the dark, secret ways of your flesh,
And I'll teach you to dance in the rain.

Ah, you're lost in yourself, and it's perfectly clear
That you don't care if I live or die,
But you're breathing a little bit faster.
So am I. So am I.

I am clapped-out and rusty, at least second-hand,
And I'm not what I once used to be,
But I've never seen anything like you before.
Won't you move a bit closer to me?

by Richard Charles

Mutuality

I am young and he is old,
I give him sex, he gives me gold,
In this there is no sacrifice
We both can well afford the price.

Sneer who will, our mutual gain
Outweighs the moralist's disdain,
We have a contract, he and I,
Secure until the day we die.

I serve him in his dwindling years,
He frees me from pecuniary fears,
Arrangements such as ours pre-date
Our less than generous welfare state.

by Philip A Nicholson

Sugar Daddy – A Warning

"It could be an acquired taste,"
I comforted myself. With haste
I sprang into his shrivelled arms,
Aiming to cash in on my charms.

I took him for a ride, they say,
And that was true, quite literally;
But lying next that fragile frame,
Brought feelings I could not quite name.

He gave his wealth, he gave his heart;
(His friends gave me the name of tart).
And now he's dead I'm richer still –
Sole benefactress of his Will.

So why bereft? Why falling tears?
My plan worked perfectly, my dears.
But I would give back all my store
To hear his gentle voice once more.

by Isabel Vincent

Father

Three years he looked at that infernal stream
The wise called Styx, although its name was Somme,
Envied the dead, until he heard them scream
Out in the devastated No Man's Land
Where mud and pain made every shot and bomb
Explicit in its murderous reprimand.

After an armistice was engineered
Living was sweet and bright the morning air;
Back at the bank from which he volunteered
He worked another twenty years of peace,
Married, and had a son; nothing, I swear
Lessened the comfort of his great release.

Out of a war and its debasing mess
Had come a kindness and a constant calm;
I was his son, and saw his happiness
Even another war could not disturb;
His thoughts were thankful, and his ways a psalm,
The sweetness of his fatherhood superb.

by Paul Griffin

Diana Re-clothed

Diana Rivestita

Weary from the toils of hunting,
Actaeon stood breathless, panting,
Left his hounds upon the mountain
To seek out a shady fountain;
Came upon a cave's arcana
Where he glimpsed the nude Diana.
Ah, too late to ask forgiveness
Of the venerated huntress!

Thinking him some hapless suitor
She destroyed his gaze with water.
From his forehead antlers sprouted,
Actaeon in terror shouted,
But his cry, a feeble bleating,
Reached the hounds that he'd been leading
Over plains and peaks and passes;
Now they ripped the stag to pieces.

Clad again, demure Diana
Summoned to her, nymphs and fauna;
Walking where she tossed the water,
She stepped past the trace of slaughter;
With her servants in attendance
Off she sped with cold indifference.
Goddess glimpsed in all her glory!
Trust the Sun to tell the story.

by Frank McDonald

Sandwiches

Afternoon Tea – 1917

All that Sunday she sits by the window
And anxiously looks down the lane,
Perhaps he'll have disembarked early
And boarded the ten o'clock train.

She'll have spent most of Saturday baking,
(Her sponge cakes and scones are a dream),
Bought a fresh two-pound loaf from the baker's,
And the farmer's supplied her with cream.

Neat triangles of bread light and crustless
With cucumber sliced wafer thin
She has lovingly laid on bone china,
Translucent like her parchment skin.

When the clock on the mantel chimes seven,
And there's barely a glow in the grate,
She abandons her self-imposed vigil,
Sure her son won't have left it so late.

Now the bread is curled up at the corners,
The cucumber shrivelled and dry,
A buff envelope lies there unopened,
And a tear gently falls from her eye.

by Brian Mitchell

Social Sandwich

Since growing deaf and poor at conversation
I know myself, in social life, a bore,
So try to keep withdrawn from circulation
To seek a tête á tête but nothing more.

Yet sometimes find I'm sandwiched in a trio,
Unhappily *de trop* and ill at ease,
To sit in silence envying the brio
With which my neighbours chatter while I freeze.

They talk across me, after briefly greeting
The one they know unlikely to cut in.
I long to leave but any other seating
Might be as bad and so I stay shut in.

A sandwich filling can remain unnoticed
But would be noticed should it rise and go.
Better, then, stay in place and make no protest,
Shrink in my chair and let the gossip flow.

What would another do, I sometimes question.
What might a book on etiquette advise?
Nothing has come my way as a suggestion
Other than wearing sandwich-spread disguise.

by Griselda Scott

Figs

Figs

Come, let me touch your sweetness, handsome love!
This secret seed-purse in its tender skin,
Soft to the touch, packed to its hidden brim
With potency, enchants me. Look, above
Our heads the fig-leaves break the evening sun
With shady patterning, and when the cool
Of moonlight comes and we are slaked and full
With our abundance, when we have begun
To fail, I'll gather figs and watch you eat.
Jealous of them within your bearded mouth,
I'll kiss you, taste the spilled seed on your breath,
Touching your lips with tongue-tip, I'll entreat
More love. The fig's poor purse is split and gone
But your sweet power to spend goes on and on.

by Alison Prince

Fig Leaves Forever

From Praxiteles we all know
That Greeks were not ashamed to show
Parts which, later, Gian Bernini
Carved so delicately teeny.

Pulchritude by coy Canova
Was censored by his draping over
Particulars that Moore implied
In gaping holes, left open wide.

But what I wonder do you think
When you see those men by Frink?
Hirsute in black and matted fur
They leave you little to infer.

The shock of David's great big cock,
Carved up there in solid rock,
Threatens all below who stare,
Upwards, in the hallowed air.

But some, who patronise the arts,
Would much prefer that private parts
Are hidden tidily away;
Not in your face and on display.

So, now our art is purified
In tanks filled with formaldehyde;
Thus, up to date, we can ensure
That Eve's fig leaf shall still endure.

by Mick Humphreys

Fowler Revisited

Don't be conservative! Gather some moss,
Count unhatched chickens and value a toss,
Go for those birds in the bush, make a leap
Over a chasm with no prior peep,
Buy the odd poke – take a risk on the pig.
    Give a fig!

Who wants an early worm? Shadow the sun,
Call all men happy, then have bullish fun
In every china shop, cry if you will
Over spilt milk, don't give grist to the mill,
Break free of fashion – tell *them* what you dig.
    Give a fig!

Have the first laugh not the last – be perverse:
Teach that old dog some new tricks, make a purse
Out of sows' ears, while you give them your pearls,
Cancel the betting on good little girls -
Tell them bad wolves of to-day aren't so big.
    Give a fig!

by Alanna Blake

Figs

In ancient Capua, one sunny day -
We had a singularly brief affair . . .
(Was the sex good or bad and did we care?)
I saw the ruins and he had his way,
Upon his Fiat's reclining seats we lay.
What was his name? What colour was his hair?
Blonde, brown or black? What interests did we share?
I don't remember much so cannot say.
Yet certain memories stay with me still -
The laden tree we found upon a hill,
Beside an empty farmhouse with a broken gate.
We pulled down branches, plucked the fruit and ate
Ripe figs split open in the sun, pink pulp
Was sucked from skins and swallowed at a gulp.

by Fiona Pitt-Kethley

Virtue? A Fig

In the deserted orchard where we wandered
Sharp sunlight splintered down through lichened twigs.
Beside the ancient wall a fig tree squandered
Over the grass its litter of split figs.

Innocents we were, and – just as tricky –
Still shy with one another. But how good
Those ripe seductive figs; how sweetly sticky
Our two mouths, crammed with strange exotic food.

Adam was tempted by an apple, merely.
What if a fig had been the fruit Eve chose?
Offered that globe of yielding flesh, how nearly
An angel would have fallen, heaven knows!

So why did *we* not fall? The prohibitions
Planted in us stunted wilder pleasure . . .
Then, I had foolish, naïve inhibitions;
Now, I have heartsickness beyond all measure.

Perhaps the lives we chose since then were fitter
Than those we might have lived – by whose design?
The taste of figs must always now be bitter:
I am not yours; you never will be mine.

by Jane Falloon

Water

Mermaid

I met her on the seashore when I tried to read her mind.
But then you see, I found, it was – not of the human kind.

Her head was full of herrings' heads and broken lobster-claws.
And things that live quite happily, beyond our native shores.

Perhaps it was the seaweed that she wore around her hips,
Or twirled into her salty hair with pinkish 'Kirby-Grips'.

I asked her once, I asked her twice, I asked her once again.
And this is what she said to me, one morning in the rain.

"You need to look for dolphins' teeth and search for mermaids' curls
And thread them into necklaces for newly-wedded girls.

But if you find an oyster shell, then throw it out to sea.
And when it floats upon the waves, then you shall marry me."

I asked again, this time in words I thought she'd understand.
She smiled and wriggled sideways, leaving scale prints in the sand.

And now as I grow older, with the passing of the years,
I often ask the question, "Why did God put salt in tears?"

WATER ─────────────

So, by the weeping ocean's side
A star-fish stranded by the tide,
Or shells of iridescent blue
Remind me of the creature who

Was standing on the seashore when I tried to read her mind.
But her thoughts were underwater, with the fishes — and their kind.

by Laurence Joyce

Aqua Viva

I am the endless tides of time,
I flowed through pre-Silurian slime,
Through dust, through rust, through grit, through grime
Flow on, flow on forever.

I am the Bible's ancient Flood,
I am the rains, the sleet, the mud.
Within your veins, I'm in your blood.
Flow on, flow on forever.

I slaked the thirst of emperors
And quenched the sweat of slaves.
Yet man's eternal tyranny
Has never tamed my waves.
I cushion babes within the womb,
And seep through mouldy graves.
Flow Rubicon, flow Amazon,
Flow on and on and free.

I am the storm, the tempest's brew,
The mists of dawn, the evening dew.
I'm sixty-five per cent of *you*.
I am the sea,
Eternally . . .
Flow on, flow on forever.

by Fergus Gwynplaine MacIntyre

Truly, Madly and Deeply

There's a whiteness on the water
As the wind on evening tide,
Soft braids the moonlit tresses
Of a maid who'll be a bride.

She's waiting for her lover
Who had sailed six months before,
Though vowing he would wed her
On return to England's shore.

Each sail she spied so eagerly,
Yet all of them passed by.
So morning came to afternoon,
Then cruel dusk strained her eye.

But still she prayed, and shivered
As the child within her stirred,
And waved the promised lantern
When e'er a ship was heard.

With fading hope she screamed his name
Across the foam-flecked sound,
Then wildly laughed when she was told
Her sailor love was drowned.

But now she's gone to find him
In the sea where no one cares,
And the whiteness on the water
Is the wedding gown she wears.

by Robert Jules Vincent

Hunting

Ottery St. Mary

Underneath the Blackdown Hills there settles out of sight,
an ancient beast that sleeps all year, and wakes on Bonfire Night.
What kind of beast he is that haunts the Otter Vale alone,
few can tell, for few have seen, and fewer still have known,
whilst searching in the narrow lanes or in the market place,
how many times they heard his voice, and looked upon his face.
But every year they come from every corner of the shire,
to seek his lair, and celebrate the festival of fire.

Ten expeditions gathered the equipage of the chase –
a bowl of pitch to trap the beast, and fire to light his face,
and strengthened casks to keep him in, tar-lined and tinder dry,
padded coats and padded gloves to hoist the barrels high;
strips of cord to bind the hair and grease to guard the skin,
hand-held cannon, primed to give the signal to begin.
Four hours passed, no nook was left for watchers to explore,
but I had not seen anything I had not seen before.

The doorways now were empty, and the cobbled streets were bare,
the smoke still hung on blackened walls, the tar still burnt the air;
the smell of cider lingered at the entrance to each inn,
the quarry still alert without, the hounds asleep within.
A thousand times, a thousand more, I walked the weathered way,
with thoughts that filtered festive night, and eyes that painted day.
I watched all night with fading hope, beneath the speckled dome,
and just before the morning light, I saw him scurry home.

by Vincent L Smith

Quarry

I know what the deer knows: that beauty is no shield
For the softness that his arrows long to wound:
He lifts his bow, the herd is still, the fairest in the field
Falls stricken, proud and tearless to the ground.
She'd turned to him before he aimed, he'd drop now if he could,
But man is born a hunter and her face stirs up his blood.

I know what the hare knows: that terror blinds the brain
And the pack will have no pity on my fear;
The leveret may speed in play but fleetness is in vain
When the courser's cry unnerves its practised ear.
The kindest heart acts out of kind when conquest is his goal,
For man is born a hunter and the race runs through his soul.

I know what the fox knows: that slyness is my life,
Though my cunning turns the killing into sport,
For the creature that need never heed the thrust of butcher's knife
Is carved – to blood the novice, when it's caught.
And he, in turn, will never rest in peace with all he owns,
For man is born a hunter and the chase is in his bones.

by Barbara Daniels

A Hunt for Immortality

I numbered in my mind the human race
In all its millions upon the earth
And thought not only does each year replace
The cull of death, but more than needed birth
Augments the total. We should walk on bones,
Find quarries full of flesh, fill lakes with blood,
Make concrete out of skulls instead of stones
And pray for cleansing by another Flood.

I studied all the teachings of the Church
'Til I could hold my own in hot debate
Then started on my not yet ended search:
To know what, after death, will be man's fate.
Worldwide I travelled, questioned learned men
Whose strange beliefs were hard to comprehend.
In different tongues the answer came again
Assuring me: Death comes not as the end.

I asked for evidence but they had none,
No vocal apparition, nothing said.
Of revenants and ghosts no single one
Describes the circumstance of being dead.
I found a legend priests have always taught:
That black eternal night is not a threat.
Against all reason hope is in the thought
That there may be a resurrection yet.

by D Shepherd

Cat

Cagney the camouflaged, Cagney the purposeful,
Mutedly mottled to blend with the ground.
Sandy brown, black stippled, no way symmetrical,
Formlessly undefined, not to be found.

Crouched in an ambush, with pent-up ferocity
Twitching her tail tip, she waits for the voles;
Dealer of death to such small squeaking creatures
That quiver and scuttle in vain for their holes.

Silent by starlight she slips through the scenery,
Feline invisible – no sight, no sound.
Bane of all rodents, the killer, the Kali,
The paramount predator, huntress uncrowned.

by Prue Sheldon

Frailty

Alzheimer's

my sons a bigshot back in quincy mass
he never calls ive lost my teeth what time
is it my daughters looking after me
here in this place wrapped in a tissue i'm

afraid though of the man i think he is
my son in law its hard to breathe did i
put on my patch my ankles hurt my chest
i sent him to three colleges i lie

awake at night and say my rosaries
i worked for sixty years i was alone
after their father died nobody came
was that the door he cant pick up the phone

although i sent him to three colleges
my son the doctor never calls i want
to pee wrapped up in tissue paper i
cant feel my patch my ankles hurt i cant

remember if we went to church this week
what days tomorrow what was yesterday
i dont remember what they call this place
cant breathe cant sleep cant feel my patch i'll say

my rosaries and pray she finds my teeth
wrapped up or in the jar in paradise
i'll not meet bigshot or the other one
the son in law with murder in his eyes

by Norman Bissett

Frailty?

She went to do her shopping at a geriatric trot;
It didn't take her long because she couldn't buy a lot.
She needed shoes, she needed coal, the milk bill must be paid
And only on the groceries could savings still be made.

The three lads moved in round her when she stopped to tie a lace;
They blacked her eye and broke her arm and cut her mouth and face.
They tossed her handbag with contempt over a nearby fence,
Not even bothering to take the few remaining pence.

The young policeman trying for a statement was amazed:
She spoke so very firmly, although clearly she was dazed.
"They're only kids; they've no home life; their world is full of rage -
They don't have the advantages that I had at their age."

by Isabel Vincent

Bliss

Bliss?

Some look for bliss in solitude
And some in love's embrace;
Some seek delight in luscious food,
Some in a baby's face.
Wordsworth found it in his youth,
A sojourner in France,
But Gray revealed the greatest truth,
That bliss is ignorance.

No one can tell what lies in wait
Or how a dream will end,
For many a man shows off his mate
To lose her to a friend.
The bliss that's of the purest kind
Can vanish like the dew
For what at twenty stirs the mind
May bore at sixty-two.

And in a fleeting world like this
We lose the things we crave;
Our only hope of lasting bliss
Must lie beyond the grave.

The cat that slumbers on my quilt
Asks neither 'how?' nor 'why?'
Untouched by grief, regret or guilt
She's happier than I.

by O Smith

Bliss is an Empty Room

Bliss is an empty room, a curtain glowing
yellow as sunlight, in the seawind blowing;
nothing else there
but a table, a chair,
a lamp to give light
and a bed for the night.

All now is done, all the to-ing and fro-ing,
all things sorted out for the selling or stowing,
all tidied and swept,
only special things kept,
things that we knew
would remind us of you.

Bliss is a quiet end and a joyful going
softly in sleep with the ebb tide gently flowing.
You would always maintain
those who love meet again.
Who am I to decry
a hope held so high?

Bliss is the harvest brought home, the reaping of sowing.
The promise has always been there but yet no foreknowing
that all will be well.
Time only will tell.
I will take things on trust –
for your sake I must.

by Angela Greenhill

Beginning of Bliss?

It is sad when you've passed all those active years
And your future is plainly so small:
Your mind is more open to all kinds of fears
As events of the past you recall.
You think of the day when love's pain first arrived,
Each hour incomplete without Her:
Each day when a meeting was somehow contrived,
With the pulse of strong passion astir.
Time moves on apace, there come children to feed,
There's a house and a garden to tend:
There's the cash you must earn to provide what you need
To increase, to maintain and to mend.
Then the children grow up and must do their own thing,
Making lives for themselves otherwhere,
And it's then you begin to feel some of the sting
As their lives you no longer share.
Then it's 'Grandpa' and 'Grandma' and baby-sit days,
With age creeping on ever more
To retirement and leisure, being put out to graze,
'Til the end of life knocks at your door.
Then you look back in wonder at all the years passed
That have brought you from childhood to this,
And you know that your time must be near to its last . . .
Is this the beginning of bliss?

by Rannoch Melville Russell

Two Faces

Unfinished Business

The board will be coming to see me today
So I'll have to be careful I'm told,
But reviewing my case they will see by my face
I deserve to be free and paroled.

So they read the reports and see I've behaved
Then ask if I've any complaints.
I smile and say none, though it isn't much fun
When your arms are strapped tight in restraints.

I show them a face which is thoughtful and kind
And ready to start a new life,
But the face that I hide is the one deep inside
Which I keep in my room with my knife.

"Your wife and your family still love you," they lie,
"The hospital says they are fine."
But a voice in my head says they all should be dead,
Which was more by bad luck than design.

Still that razor-sharp blade is just biding its time
As the voice tells me what I must do,
But the board must have heard for again I'm referred
And my last chance of freedom falls through.

But Christmas is coming, they'll tell her it's safe,
So she'll bring all the children as well.
I'll be quick and explain that they won't feel much pain
As I silence those voices from Hell.

by Robert Jules Vincent

The Face Below

While drawing nudes in Art School I could see
A second face on each stare back at me,
With navel nostrils, twinkling nipple eyes,
A grinning crease where torso meets the thighs.
Some looked quite glum, while others gave a smile;
Males stuck their tongues out with expressions vile.
Often, a model on a Windsor chair
Wearing a string of pearls and well-coiffed hair,
Looked too demure a type of woman to know
The bearded lady smirking down below.

by Fiona Pitt-Kethley

Two-faced Streets

Is the child down your street with the locked-away smile
abused? If you knew, would you care,
and then set the smile free with your brave man's truth?
Or net-curtain the face of despair?

Are the shouts from over the road just part
and parcel of family life?
Or is the nice bloke with the permanent smile
beating up a downtrodden wife?

Is the white-haired old lady, who lives all alone,
a street-angel, a kindly old dear?
Or a house-devil vixen who's ruined the lives
of her children, who never come near?

Is the smart pin-striped gent, whose persona just oozes
family values and such,
the same guy who kerb-crawls for what he can't get
from a wife who rejects every touch?

Each street has two faces – one smiling and brave:
the other – screwed up by the past -
fleshed out by illusion; with madness and fears
simply veiled by a paper-thin mask.

by Jenny Proom

Children From Hell

Case for the Defence

Children, from Hell? No, no, you've got it wrong,
Children are sent from Heaven. They are spun
From star-dust, honey-dew and angel-song,
And innocent as daisies, every one.
You have my word on it that this is so;
Some of my friends have children, and I know.

by Noel Petty

The New Intake

Do they roll up to the College
Each one thirsting after knowledge?
Is it thoughts of gaining wisdom that impel?
Are they braced for three years' toil?
Will they burn the midnight oil?
Will they bend themselves to study? Will they Hell!

Can they write clear, simple prose?
If asked, can they compose
Declaratory sentences which tell
What thoughts they'd like to voice
On some topic of their choice?
Can they write a decent essay? Can they Hell!

Is their numeracy sound?
Do they have a solid ground
In Geometry and Algebra as well?
Do they have at least a notion
Of the basic Laws of Motion?
Do they know what DNA is? Do they Hell!

Do they know that they've been fooled?
That they're hopelessly ill-schooled?
That the system is a comprehensive sell?
They've been told that standards rise -
Have they fallen for such lies?
May those who so deceived them burn in Hell.

by M Hammerton

Ye shall know them by their Fruits

Children, miracles of nature,
Precious gifts from God above,
Human seedlings, needing nurture,
Needing care and needing love.

Those who think the young are devils
To be tamed and taught the rules,
Beaten, bored into submission,
Are but spiteful, frightened fools.

Jesus was a little baby.
So was Hitler, so was I.
Born in blood and pain, defenceless,
Innocent and bound to die.

Made from genes of Mum and Daddy,
Watching, storing every day.
Shitty kids have shitty parents.
There is nothing more to say.

by Richard Charles

In Praise of Plumpness

The Long and the Short

To launch his population plan
God made a roly-poly man,
Satan not to be outdone
Produced a long and lanky one.
The first became the most revered
The other, less adored than feared,
For on the whole the stout are not
Too fond of stratagem and plot
While fatefully the restless 'lean'
Are prone to agitate and scheme,
But though we praise the plump we must
Remember that all comes to dust,
And when the flesh falls from the frame
The bones beneath look much the same.

by Philip A Nicholson

Rubenesque

Rubens paints perfect pleasure: love of flesh
in celebration of a woman's form,
his earthly worship of the blushing, warm
plumpness of pinks and carmine, seeing fresh

promises in soft folds above her hips,
her sweet voluptuousness of glowing skin
luxuriantly bathed in light, and in
her laughing face her round and welcoming lips.

Goddess or wife, his women fill their space
ample and radiant as a damask rose,
regal in stance, relaxed in formal pose,
plump as silk cushions, arched in supple grace

and generous and ripe as August's sun;
solid and sensuous, innocent of spite,
women whose sole existence is delight,
whose joy and careless beauty yields to none.

by D A Prince

In Praise of Plumpness

For me no skinny little frump
with bones like dagger points.
Give me a lady who is plump
with smoothly covered joints.

I can't resist a dimpled knee,
and firm pink cheeks and lips.
A silky-soft skin that's for me,
all over ample hips.

Ah! Rubens' ladies; what delight,
big-breasted, bare and bold.
Keep Lowry's matchsticks out of sight,
there's nothing there to hold.

Thin feels like half of her's not there.
Plump's *always* gorgeous, clothed or bare.

by John Kerkhoven

'Ripeness is All'

No poet ever praised a shrivelled pear
Or matched his mistress with a wrinkled prune;
No hostess worth the name would ever dare
To serve a pudding like a pricked balloon.

For fruits and puddings, all good things on earth
That bring contentment and a thankful heart
Are chiefly loved for amplitude of girth,
And in this scheme we too should play a part.

Proud Caesar had no little cause to fear
Conspiring Cassius, treacherous and lean,
For skinny folk, it's manifestly clear,
Are full of malice, bitterness and spleen.

You have, dear sir, no reason to abhor
Your 'fair round belly' and your double chin;
These are the features all your friends adore
So pray to God you never will be thin.

And madam, too, to slim is ill-advised
For no one loves a scraggy, spiteful frump;
Venus de Milo wasn't undersized;
Stay as you are, warm, comforting and plump.

by O Smith

I Need no Shadow Whispering in my Ear

I need no shadow whispering in my ear
That I am mortal; there is little fear
Now, in my final quarter, that I may
Forget the culmination of the play.
And when the mirror offers back my stare,
I do not wish to see reflected there
The wide sardonic grin
Of the skull beneath the skin.

And when my lover gently peels away
The kindly artifices of the day
I do not want the scaffolding made plain,
Socket and sinew, vertebra and vein.
I know too painfully our mortal state
And need no lines of rib-bone to narrate
The fatalistic story
Of our joint memento mori.

Show me no bones, no ridges, corners, ends,
For now I would know flesh that swoops and bends
In sinuous cycloid, elegant ellipse;
Flesh that is yielding to the finger tips,
As soft as summer, pourable as cream,
That lets me, willingly deluded, dream
Of never-ending laughter
And happy-ever-after.

by Noel Petty

Frolic

Bibliophrolic

I'm feeling rather naughty – let's uncork the *Oxford Shortie,*
Put the effervescent essence of *Britannica* on ice;
With such vintage verbal vino we can have a proper beano
And, with deference to Reference, now wouldn't that be nice!
We can shed our inhibitions in those heady old editions
Such as *Brewer's Phrase and Fable* – *that'll* make the party swing –
And with liberal libations out of *Humorous Quotations*
And a chorus from *Thesaurus,* we can make the rafters ring!
Oh, the world is free of hassle with a *Collins* or a *Cassell!*
Is the *Chambers* nicely *chambré?* then I don't mind if I do.
With a *Webster* or a *Longman* life's a lyric for a song, man,
And I think I'm getting slowly alcoholier than you.
Bring the *Scholes* and bring the *Drabble!* I'll take on the world at Scrabble!
Bring the *Partridge* and the *Fowler* – they're not strictly for the birds!
Bring me *Homer! Aristotle!* let me broach another bottle
For a toast to *Doctor Johnson* and the wacky world of words!

by Joan Butler

Frolic

He was a little dancing bear
Performing daily with the show.
From birth he'd travelled with the Fair
And he had nowhere else to go.

One day his pen was not shut tight;
He pushed the door and sniffed the air
And ambled off into the night
Without a purpose, anywhere.

News of his venture travelled fast:
Ferocious Bear Escapes From Cage,
And people heard the words, aghast:
The Killer Bear's on the Rampage.

They came upon him quite by chance
Unfed, not knowing where to roam.
He gladly broke into his dance
And hoped that they would take him home.

Needless to say, they shot him dead.
"We faced the brute and felt no fear
Although he snarled and growled", they said.
His little frolic cost him dear.

by D Shepherd

Still Frolicking After All These Years

Morning sun made soft by summer haze
Above a sea of opalescent silk
A beach as smooth and shiny as the glaze
Upon the yellow beakers for our milk,
An invitation through an open sash
For frolics through the happy hours ahead,
A glorious mix of sand and shells and splash
Until, tired out, we'd gladly go to bed.

Arms and legs made brown by sun and wind,
Eyes made bright by lashings of fresh air,
Perhaps we were by nature then thick skinned,
Immune to burns and brittleness of hair.
Too young for sex, but not too young to play
Rough and tumble on the springy turf
That insulated sand dunes where we lay
To watch the boats that rode the Cornish surf.

Now I lie back in my bath and dream,
Whilst making waves and ripples with my toe,
Of days of candy sugar and ice cream,
Of innocence and frolics years ago.
Now I walk, too dignified to run,
Too staid for leaps, make others jump instead,
But though I seem quite frolic-less, no one
Can stop the daily frolics in my head.

by Katie Mallett

Frolic

In my heart are young maidens and laughter
And maypoles and music and dance.
There are hampers from Fortnum and Mason
And exquisite bottles from France.
Round the pole men are chasing the maidens,
As I would if I had the chance.

In my head I know this doesn't happen -
Though the young ones are frolicsome still,
The lute's given way to the disco
While tablets are taken for thrill,
And the maidens don't need so much chasing -
They're content to rely on the Pill.

In my body, alas, there's no question
Of donning the cap and the bells.
A crossword is my recreation
Though my brain may be losing its cells.
BUT the sight of a maiden in springtime
Is a pleasure that age never quells.

by John Wedge

Fish

To a Goldfish

Goldfish in suburban pond,
Do you ever look beyond
The concrete bounds of your domain
Where you effortlessly glide
Hour by hour from side to side
And up and down and back again?

Do you ever dream a dream
Of basking in a limpid stream
And drifting with the current's flow,
Or take a moment to surmise
What alien earthbound region lies
Outside the watery world you know?

Perhaps it's best to be secure,
Far from temptation's cunning lure;
For here you're safe from angler's bait
And savage pike's voracious jaw
And heron's beak and otter's claw,
Within your pool inviolate.

And we, like you, by walls confined,
May plan adventures of the mind
In distant lands or outer space;
But we, too, have our daily round
That keeps our feet upon the ground
In one suburban place.

by O Smith

Fish-Eye

Up in the dazzling dryness, mayflies dance,
Tempting with tastiness all those who dare
Leap through the world's skin into empty air.
The brave will trust their blood-stream, take their chance,
Fall back in gasping glory. Danger brings
Delight. Cruise through the cool, reed-pillared halls
In triumph – but beware. A shadow falls
Across the sparkling ceiling, then outflings
A hiss of line. Watch for the sharp-hooked fly,
The fighting, hopeless drag to air-choked death.
Just once, a giant beast of boots and breath
Plunged through the winter ice, lost to his sky,
And now the great pike, lord of the deepest stones,
Swims through the white cathedral of his bones.

by Alison Prince

Fish

On funereal marble slabs laid out,
Lifeless, inert, the cold cadavers lie.
Hake, halibut and cod, salmon and trout,
Stare sightlessly with blank and glassy eye.
Dead fish – can anything more dead appear?
And yet, what life was theirs, what beauty, grace!
A spawning salmon, leaping up the weir;
A shoal's switch of direction or of pace,
Shared instantly, as if one life controlled
Them all; the rainbow throng about the reef;
The luminescent monsters of the cold
And sunless deep. Past measure, past belief,
Life's myriad forms in rivers, lakes and seas.
Which come to mind – those on the slab, or these?

by John Lord

Trout Tickling

Turf bright and smooth, shaved by the grazing sheep,
Bracken and tumbled stones, and a broad stream
Poured from the cleft fell, in a splash of cream
Hurled over rock till the last graceful leap
Suddenly into calm and clean and deep . . .
Under its curving banks the fat trout dream.
Above, the serious children wait and scheme,
Then flex their eager fingers while they creep,
Flattened and shadowless, up to the cool brim.
My heart bangs, bangs – but I must hold my breath,
Nothing betray me as I wriggle on . . .
I reach the edge – I stretch my hand beneath
The overhang, and trembling, feel for him.
He's there! I've got him! Slide, twist, flip – he's gone.

by Mary Holtby

Kith and Kin

Losing Her

You are trying to forget how much you loved her,
As you watch her disappearing day by day,
As her skin recoils each time you try to touch her,
And the eyes that sparkled fade and look away.

You pay the bills and wonder if she's happy,
You cook the food, you do the things you must,
But the little voice that once rang out with laughter
Dismisses you in tones of faint disgust.

You remember all the days you spent together,
When you were at the centre of her world,
When she ran to you and trusted you completely,
And she was Daddy's precious little girl.

Her photographs hang all around your bedroom,
There's the card she made for you when she was three,
And a tiny pair of tights behind a bookcase
Can break your heart and bring you to your knees.

You say you're not the first, all this is nature.
You think you'll come to terms with it quite soon.
But the past is warm and soft and brightly-coloured,
And the future's like the dark side of the moon.

You eat, you work, you sleep, you keep on breathing,
You serve out your life sentence as you should,
Still trying to forget how much you loved her,
And knowing that your best is gone for good.

by Richard Charles

Kith and Kin

Joe is spreading out his bed-roll in a doorway on the Strand,
As the theatre-goers rush to catch the play.
It's only seven-thirty, but he's drunk, depressed and dirty,
And he's seen enough of London for the day.

Mother muses at the mirror, brushing back her bleached-blond hair,
Wondering when her evening client will appear.
She finds it rather funny that she now turns tricks for money -
Once she did it just for cigarettes and beer.

Now his father's chanting vespers at an abbey near Turin.
(He lied about his past to get a place.)
All those years he spent at Broadmoor made him wish he'd lived abroad more,
Just before he meets his maker face to face.

Sister Cindy tweaks her nipples till they stand out proud and pink
And prepares herself for yet another take.
It's afternoon in LA and the studio's a mêlée
Of pornographers and agents on the make.

Joe is dreaming of his childhood and the fun he used to have
Before his younger sister moved abroad.
His mother groans with pleasure in her mercenary leisure
And his father lifts his eyes unto the Lord.

by Laurence Joyce

Quietness

Stranded

I walk out on the mud and remember the past,
As the tide washes over the wrecks.
You were fearless and wise, you had wonderful eyes.
I was lonely and crazy for sex.

And you fed me on stories, seduced me with songs,
Drunk on dreams, wild with passion and tears,
Promised Paris in Spring, then you gave me a ring,
Made me pregnant and brought me down here.

But the future was ours, we were only pretending
To live like the common folk did,
As we worked for our pay, just survived day to day,
Got a mortgage and brought up the kids.

Now the house is quite quiet, the children are gone,
I rise early and go to bed late,
And you sit over there in your favourite chair,
And I don't feel a thing, only hate.

I walk out on the mudflat and gaze at the wreck
No one bothered to try to refloat:
Half-submerged, half-forgotten, paint peeled, timbers rotten,
Your beautiful pea-green boat.

by Richard Charles

A Visit

My house is *spooky*. That is what they say,
The young ones, when they briefly come and stay.
What *spooks* them is the disconcerting lack
Of throbbing music, all and every day,
Their necessary fuel, their backing track.

To me it seems discourteous at best
To ask Vivaldi, Schubert and the rest,
Or even Chumbawamba for that matter,
To strut their stuff above our noise and jest,
To try to reach us through a fog of chatter.

But when at last the motors disappear
The silence seems to echo in my ear.
I try to read, but somehow cannot block
Out from my mind that clichéd sound of fear,
The unrelenting ticking of the clock.

Absurd, of course. And I can exorcise
That ghost: remove the clock. To my surprise
The beat grows stronger when its source is gone,
The mind asserting what the ear denies.
Perhaps, I think, I'll put a record on.

by Noel Petty

The Muse of Silence

Into the glade the minstrel hastes
Lays ringing in his ears.
He swiftly draws a makeshift score
And transcribes all he hears.

The maestro twirls his bushy curls
And pens the trumpet blasts,
But as he darts the violins' part
A shady shape glides past.

Quietness falls, the rhythm stalls,
The notes slink off in fear,
A hush descends, the clamour ends
As Tacita draws near.

"O minstrel wild, Commotion's child,
Thy brassy thoughts offend
Becalm thy mind, thy chords unwind
And I'll thy ballad mend.

To thee faint flutes and lilting lutes
Bespeak tranquillity,
While soundless swings of swallows' wings
Are thunderclaps to me.

But put aside thy louder side
And score as I suggest."
The minstrel marks her wise remarks
And fills his staves with rests.

by Caspian Richards

The Party's Over Now

The final guest has gone, though only just,
My ears still ringing from his bellowed thanks,
"Great party – huge success – you gotta – must -
You, 'n' – whoever – come next week to mine . . ."
He lurched and stumbled down the stairs. Ah well,
At least it shows I didn't stint on wine.

Or stint myself – but now my head is clear,
Clear as the night – and I can see a star . . .
It's peaceful on this balcony out here,
All hushed. Not silent, cities never are
With so much seething life – but sleeping now.
A purr from time to time, from someone's car . . .

A few hours on, that purr will be a roar!
But now this little space of calm is mine,
Between what lies ahead and went before.
So still and quiet . . . a distant plume of smoke
Is barely ruffled by untroubled air.
The quietness enfolds me like a cloak.

Tomorrow's all too near – but for tonight
I'll gather up its folds and hold them tight.

by Pamela Martin

Choirboys

Song of Innocence

The choir stands still and reverent in lines of black and white,
Each angel face, each virgin soul bathed in God's holy light.
The widow's eyes mist over as she bows her head to pray
For the little boy from Number 10 who vanished yesterday.

(Out on the spit a child is lying naked in the mud.
His eyes are wide with terror and his lips are caked in blood.
His limbs are stiff and twisted, there are skewers through his hands.
A fishing boat heaves to, and someone wades towards the land.)

In God's great House the pure soprano voices fill the air,
The Holy Spirit comforts all who suffer and despair,
And no one sees the smirk as someone catches someone's eye
And sweetly sings of pastures green the quiet waters by.

(The murder team works urgently against the rising tide,
A journalist asks, "Is it true the child was crucified?"
The fisherman just whimpers, they are treating him for shock.
They have wrapped him in a blanket but the shaking will not stop.)

"The Grace of God go with you all for ever more. Amen."
The widow shuffles home and looks across at Number 10.
The squad car has arrived, she hopes the child is safe and well.
The lady PC bites her lip, the policeman rings the bell.

by Richard Charles.

Elegy for Choirboys

I knew them all, their rosy faces bright
Above their ruffs like apples on a plate,
Their weekday imperfections out of sight
Beneath their surplices immaculate.

And when they sang the time itself stood still
As all that sexless purity of tone
Rose to the vaulted roof and seemed to spill
Beyond the church and reach God's very throne.

But none who listened dared to break the spell
And say that boys grow up and sing no more,
And none possessed the vision to foretell
What destinies the future held in store.

For some died on a beach in Normandy
And some fell earthwards in a blazing plane;
One died in Burma; some were lost at sea
Or on the bloody sand of Alamein.

The church still stands where once they loved to sing.
Their names live on, inscribed upon a plaque,
But who can tell the anguish that they bring
As memories long dulled come flooding back?

Now three or four old men, frail, bent and grey,
Sing on with tuneless voice and quavering tongue,
The last poor relics of a distant day.
Only the dead remain forever young.

by O Smith

Choirboys

Choirboys I've dodged as a subject for poetry,
Hoping my readers won't take it amiss;
I frequently write about how well I know a tree,
Rave about landscapes and moments of bliss,
Even embark upon themes metaphysical,
Sketch out a scene that is mildly erotic,
Hinting at heaven with sighs paradisical,
All in a tale that is brief, anecdotic.

Choirboys are difficult, funny and serious,
Curious mixtures of virtues and taints,
Voices that plunge us in matters mysterious,
Ways that exasperate all but the saints.
There, from the lips that are trilling Messiah now
Chewing-gum smears on the pew ends are seen;
Under the music that makes him perspire now
Peep out the sheets of a rude magazine.

Is he an angel, or is he a Lucifer?
What will, I wonder, his adulthood be?
Which will be dominant, hellhound or crucifer?
Can such a boy reach the top of the tree?
We too were children; the rise and the fall of us
Worried our parents: when *might* we be good?
Choirboys at least can give rapture to all of us
Instant, and deeper than ever we could.

by Paul Griffin

Evensong at Ely

The organ's music rolls across the nave,
Voices soar in harmony, sweet and clear,
With measured tread, expressions aptly grave,
Two by two the cathedral choir appears.
Long shadows trace the carvings on the stalls
Where they assemble, gowned in red and white;
We revel in their singing, quite enthralled
By angelic faces framed in candlelight.
Some hours ago they ran out on the field,
Got mud-stained, bruised and tattered, fought and won.
Now washed and brushed – all injuries concealed -
They sing the praises of God's holy Son,
Within the compass of this hallowed place,
Which rises from the fenland's soft embrace.

by Maureen A Jeffs

Passion

The Story of the Hammer and the Nail

The hammer that hung in the woodshed
Was a sturdy, young bachelor male
Whose heart was engaged in the moonlight
By a beautiful, feminine nail.

She was lying nearby on the workbench,
A creature of slender, blue light,
So polished and poised her appearance
He was smitten at once by the sight.

"You're a beautiful nail!" said the hammer.
"Let me hold you, my darling, my own;
I fear for your life and your safety
When you go in the wood all alone."

The nail did not flinch from the romance,
She said he was manly and strong,
Though a plainly steel-headed claw-hammer
She encouraged his courtship with song.

He held her, slim-waisted and tender,
And gave her a tap on the head.
"My hero, you're ever so gentle,
Now claw me, my darling," she said.

So alternately tapping and clawing
In the moonlight where nocturnals roam,
The hammer made love in the woodshed,
Reluctant to drive the nail home.

by Jonathan Pool

Naming Passion

I watched you sleep – how long I watched you sleep! -
and sensed your passion burning, fathoms deep,
and heard the breath rise, wistful, in your throat,
releasing sighs, drawn out, and each long note
hung low, a ragged echo of despair,
its melancholy flavouring the air.

Your body twitched, fell open like a book -
I read the signs, that flushed and fevered look
of someone in the throes of secret bliss,
shadowed by guilt's yawning black abyss -
our comfortable marriage undermined
by words unspoken, feelings undefined.

The thought of your departure had me scared -
this threat to the domestic life we shared,
then longing woke within me, urged me slide
beneath you to unleash that rising tide,
and you bore down, possessive flesh aflame,
but called me by some other woman's name.

by J M Harvey

First Passion

Between these mundane entries – *Went to school,*
to Mass on Sunday, Benediction too -
my mother read, *Kissed Anne Marie McCool.*
(Behind the drystone wall where daisies grew.)

My mother frowned, but I did not confess
that by the drystone wall we'd kissed and worse,
for Anne Marie pulled up her gingham dress
and let me fingertip her silken purse.

It was, in truth, our one and only kiss,
for from then on, our eyes alone would meet
to share our secret taste of carnal bliss,
in class, across the playground, in the street.

We blushed at our awakened sense of awe
and fell in line with strictures from above.
No more would Anne Marie and I explore
the wilder shores of pre-pubescent love.

Though long ago I may have thought it so,
I now no longer think of it as read:
that, of the many roads a man may go,
the road to Hell begins with girls in bed.

by Terence Reid

The Wings and the Wake

Would you savour the chance to be young again,
Looking back from your fiftieth year?
Could you bear with the passion, the heartaches and pain,
And return to the fray without fear?

Sweet memories of youth and the stirring of loins,
The flutt'ring of lashes and hearts;
Discov'ring the stud where the stocking-top joins
And the virtue of childhood departs.

Those glimpses of flesh at the throat and the waist
And the promise of softness concealed;
The token resistance to amorous haste
And the thrill of the bounty revealed.

Would you burn in the fires of forbidden love,
Reaching back for the dream that is gone?
Would you rise with your soul on the wings of the dove,
Or grow old in the wake of the swan?

Remember, Old Man, when you yearn for the dove,
With a heart ever young, ever true,
Those beautiful eyes that once shone with love
Are now just as fifty as you.

by David Rogers

My Heart Leaps Up

The Scientist

My heart leaps up when I behold
Some hapless passer-by
Transfixed with joy and wonder at
A rainbow in the sky.
"No need, good sir," I say to him
"To marvel at this sight:
The optical geometry
Is hardly recondite."

"The rays," – I draw a diagram –
"Enter the raindrop thus,
Refract, reflect, refract once more
And travel back to us.
Refraction bends each colour to
A different extent,
And there's your rainbow. Quite mundane,
Almost a non-event."

I see him quite bereft of speech
That I can thus expound
The workings of a sight he'd thought
So moving and profound.
Declining any proffered thanks
I take my way again,
To seek some other needful of
My mission to explain.

by Noel Petty

My Heart Leaps Up

The lychgate swings; I make a sudden choice
To enter hallowed ground, not pass it by.
Quite sure I wouldn't even recognise God's voice
If He should call. My heart leaps up. *But why?*

Here in the quiet churchyard towering yew
Stand timeless watch as if to sanctify
The avenues of graves that I pass through.
The shadows change; my heart leaps up. *But why?*

No sign of resurrection. In this ground
Both saints and sinners, uncomplaining, lie
And do not seem to wait the last trump's sound.
The grasses move; my heart leaps up. *But why?*

I sit inside the porch as do the least
Of God's own children, thinking they are nigh
Unto their Maker. Would it please the priest
To see me there? My heart leaps up. *But why?*

Beyond the door are canopies and thrones.
I had not thought the nave would seem so high.
What presence built into these simple stones!
I catch my breath: my heart leaps up. *But why?*

I stand and watch the east rose window filled
With stained glass saints that cross the living sky.
I hear the stone saints whisper. Lips long stilled
Tell me that every heart leaps up. And why.

by Ted Giles

The Eager Heart

The rainbow and the dragonfly,
The shifting chasmed seas,
The grandeur of the mountain heights,
The miracle of trees;
Such marvels of the universe
Excite my spirit still
And while my sense of wonder lives
I know they always will.
But now we live in times that are
Ungracious, charmless, sad,
The least of trivial blessings
Hold the power to make us glad,
And so my heart leaps up when strangers
Freely pass the time of day
Or patient smiling motorists
Sacrifice their right of way;
When I hear a politician
Frankly own that he is wrong,
I go about my business
Blithely warbling a song,
Quite ready, should a nightingale
Quite appropriately give voice,
To call upon humanity
To wholeheartedly rejoice.

by Philip A Nicholson

Lunch

Company

Feeling all alone one day
I asked myself to lunch.
"Arrive at 12 o'clock," I said,
"For a drop of home-made punch."

I tore off in the Mini
And bought some fresh crevettes,
Some salmon steaks, some Jersey royals,
Tomatoes and roquette.

All morning long I slaved away,
Preparing for my guest:
Fresh soap in the lavatory,
Old china changed for best.

I was punctual, I'll give me that,
And brought an appetite,
But, on good conversation,
I found me rather light.

We sat there in grim silence
Until the meal was done –
I was better off without me;
This wasn't any fun.

Through each and every course of lunch,
Me knocked back wine and beers
And then me started shouting,
And then broke down in tears.

LUNCH

My neighbour rang the doorbell
To check I was OK,
And when I came back to the dining room,
Myself had gone – hooray!

★

Now lunch served in a loony-bin
Is a boring, bland affair.
But I've no idea who's eating it
So I don't have to care.

by Jon Sayers

Delius Myth

There's a pub called The Paradise Garden
That's renowned for seclusion and scoff;
It was here that two star-thwarted lovers
Had decided to bump themselves off.
They arrived just as lunch was beginning
And, though hardly in prandial mood,
The sorrowful maiden suggested
'Just a bite' of pre-suicide food.
Her swain, never slow on the uptake,
Relaxed and unbuttoned his coat
(In the pocket of which were his wallet
And the following sad little note:
We can't stand the aggro no longer.
Your attitude's getting us down.
So we've come to The Paradise Garden
Where we'll jump in the river and drown).
They opted for melon *prosciutto*
Then artichoke hearts *vinaigrette,*
Some *pâté de foie,* and a *sorbet,*
Roast duckling with *pommes alumettes,*
Ice cream and a cherry *Pavlova,*
But the cheese was the ultimate straw,
For they kicked the proverbial bucket
And expired, with a groan, on the floor.
Mine host, overcome with emotion,
Crying "What will my customers think?"
Read the note, took the wallet and, pronto,
He toppled them into the drink.
Fred Delius, noting the story,
Was heard to remark, "I've a hunch
This'd make a good plot for an opera
If I miss out the scene with the lunch."
He wrote it. It's long and it's laboured

And it took him two years to compose.
And *The Walk to the Paradise Garden*
Is the only bit anyone knows.
  ENVOI
Do you yearn to pre-empt the hereafter?
Undecided which route to apply?
Have a go at a surfeit of Delius.
It's a lingering death, but you'll die.

by Joan Butler

Dejeuner des Canotiers

Straw boaters, singlets, muscles draw the eyes
to those strategically placed young men,
their self-assurance caught in lucent rays
of midday sun reflecting from the Seine.

One in particular attracts the gaze
of girls whose summer hats the painter lights –
as he picks out the glow on cheek and neck
and the spent colours of a meal's delights.

There, centred on the table's crumpled cloth
among the crumbs and empty glasses, five
bottles are underscored by falling grapes;
their vintage, though unlabelled, will survive.

The little dog will always be wet-nosed,
the wine stand waiting or be held mid-sip,
the boats will sail for ever in the heat,
the awning's orange stripes will gently dip.

The master traps a moment in deft strokes
on white-toned canvas, a bright glimpse of life.
One of these pretty demoiselles (but which?)
was destined to be Renoir's future wife.

by Alanna Blake

Building

Bring me my Tactical Nuclear Missile Launcher

We are building a modern Jerusalem
To the twin Gods of Fashion and Cool,
Where all must wear clothing adorned with the name
Of some famous and talentless fool.
And the colours and concepts and styles of last year
We abhor and reject categorically,
For consumers who buy stuff and chuck it away
Make a nation that's sound economically.

We are building a fairer society
With no room for original thought,
And no favours for freaks who are gifted or bright
Unless their vocation is sport.
And the daughters and sons of celebrity chefs
Shall be given the means to gain wealth,
From design, presentation or Art without form
Funded by tax and by stealth.

We are building all over this green, pleasant land
Little boxes of grey, white and brown,
And we fill them all up with electrical junk
And then drive off to work in the town.
And everyone's browsing and surfing the web,
Taking calls on the cellular phone,
Watching endless repeats on the cable TV,
And eating and sleeping alone.

by Richard Charles

Rebuilding

The rooks are building near the church again
despite the storms which last year almost tore
their nests apart, despite the maddening roar
of winds in frenzy. Something makes them train
loose twigs around a likely branch, a skein
of moss patiently teased – repairs, as for
a tighter hold on this year, and once more
working so reconstructing's not in vain.

We watch them build what yesterday just seemed
abandoned wreckage. With your hand on mine
once more, we map their to-and-fro campaign
against whatever this year's weather's dreamed
to test them, grateful for our private sign:
the rooks are building near the church. Again.

by D A Prince

Spare Parts

My sight unaided isn't very keen
But with my glasses I can read all right
And with another pair (though not at night)
My driving skill is all it's ever been.
I'm very slightly deaf – perhaps a touch,
But with this little gadget in the ear
You could not drop a pin but I would hear.
I really hardly need it, or not much.

I've always had good teeth, but one or two
Have let me down, so now I have a plate.
I told the dentist: better not to wait
Than carry on and find it hard to chew.
As for my knees, the Army did them in
Stamping and marching – I could hardly kneel
But these new joints I've got are stainless steel
And quite invisible beneath the skin.

My urine's now got trouble getting through.
It seems for this there's no spare parts at all.
I thought there'd be a pump they could install,
A plunger, or an Archimedes screw,
Or at the worst, in case the tubes are filled
With waste and sludge, there'd be a solvent made.
Without spare parts I'm very much afraid
I may be facing a complete re-build.

by D Shepherd

Star Gazing

Star-gazing glumly at the sky
Made the ancients ponder why,
Through those dark and boring nights
Where only rumbling flatulence
Of leaking camels round their tents
Disturbed the silent stellar lights,
Unlike the stars, mankind must die.

On the antediluvian plain
They built, attempting to explain
This mystery, vast pointing signs
In piling pyramids of stones
Not as graves for rotting bones,
But huge, eternal paradigms
Of constellations which remain.

The built great monoliths of stone
Statues, which stare at stars and roam
Whole hemispheres; an inter-net
Of petrified encircling rings
Combining wild Cambodian kings
With Norsemen, Olmecs, who connect
In cruising that celestial dome.

All modern man creates today
Are plastic domes in which to play
Whilst gazing at his feet of clay.

by Mick Humphreys

Requited Love

If I Tell You

If I tell you that I love you, will you frown
And turn away as if it's quite absurd?
Or, playing safe, pretend you haven't heard,
And leave my doubts unanswered while I drown
In those uncertainties that drag me down?
Or will your eyes burn brighter at the word,
And, some sweet sharpened senses strangely stirred,
Hold out to me love's sceptre and its crown?
But, if I tell you that I love you, it may be
That, struggling for words so hard to phrase,
You'll gather courage from my longing gaze
And new-found fervour from my fingertips,
And answer that you love me – you love me,
And I, to thank them, kiss your lovely lips.

by Martin Piper

Dante's Legacy

They married and were happy ever after.
So much for that, then. Nothing to declare.
Nothing to say about the joy and laughter,
The sympathy that two like spirits share.
Nothing about the burst of recognition,
The tingling glow of seeing it returned,
The slow unfolding journey to fruition,
The pleasing symmetry of love unspurned.

How can such easy mutual affection
Compete with yearning for a hopeless goal,
Or love that never undergoes rejection
Be ranked with starved nobility of soul?
Yes, happiness can seem a fearful bore.
And poets have a lot to answer for.

by Noel Petty

Of Love Returned

I loved you in the years you were defenceless,
Your hurt was mine and mine your secret shame;
I loved you in the moisture of your sadness
When love was joy that shouted out your name;
I envied all who breathed the air around you,
And feared the nights you did not sleep alone;
I lingered in the places where I found you,
And wished with all my heart that you would phone.

You never did. The years grew cold between us,
I learned to live with love that grew no seed;
But ah! today the scheming Fates have seen us
And here you are with everything I need.
Your lips and eyes announce you as my lover,
Your hand holds mine as I recall my pain;
My heart cries out – *I want you more than ever,*
My mind decrees I will not hurt again.

Your lips implore, encourage my forgiveness,
Your kiss is life and love thrills through my soul,
Your tears are fire that burns away my hardness;
Another word and you will break my will.
Am I a fool to follow in your shadow,
To love the love that broke my heart before?
But as we kiss the future is a meadow
Of sunlit flowers – and who can ask for more?

by Frank McDonald

Loss

And so the game ends in this rumpled bed.
Love has been shared, the long-held hopes confessed,
The privacies explored. In our post-coital rest
He quietly snores. All mystery is dead,
The sweet, uncertain magic gone. I know
He works for Scottish Gas and has false teeth
Due to a Rugby mishap, playing Leith;
The Argyll socks conceal a hammer toe,
His widowed mother lives in Pittenweem.
He loves me. That's the worst. I can't betray
His dreadful trust, though it has swept away
The unrequited romance of my dream.
The trap has sprung. It caught my wild ideal
And there he lies, abominably real.

by Alison Prince

Memory Loss

The Colour of Your Eyes

I won't forget the night we met,
Your hat, your purple cloak,
Your skin, your hair, your underwear,
The music and the smoke.
Your teeth, your lips, your fingertips,
Your throat, your breasts, your thighs,
I feel them all but can't recall
The colour of your eyes.

For want or need or lust or greed,
You said that you would stay.
The babies came, we gave them names,
And watched them drift away.
And beauty sags, and passion flags,
And magic slowly dies,
And nothing's left of love except
The colour of your eyes.

And then the day you went away,
The bitter words, the tears,
The lamplit street, the driving sleet,
Your scarf around your ears.
Now all I have are photographs
That mock and tell me lies.
Who would have bet that I'd forget
The colour of your eyes?

by Richard Charles

Oblivion for the Grieving

This is a peaceful garden. I can stand
And watch the people walk in twos and threes
Along the paths, or children hand in hand
Put flowers on the statues. There are trees
To hide the road. I don't move far from here,
Where I was standing when she went away.
She used to tell me not to disappear
When she went in a shop: so I must stay.

I always seem to look out through the glass
Of those black cars that drive in through the gate.
I see the people gather on the grass:
Then I squeeze in among the trees, and wait
Because she wasn't with me in the car.
I can't remember why. I have this fear.
They leave a heap of soil that is a scar
Among the statues. Why she brought me here
I can't remember. Friends will come for me
When it gets dark, but one of them will stay
To tell her I have gone to have my tea.

This is her picture: I can't say which way
She went. I can't remember. I'll come back
Tomorrow. When she comes she'll set me straight.
If it is raining I shall wear a mac
And bring her an umbrella. And I'll wait.

by Ted Giles

Theseus

They had the wretched Minotaur confined
Within the labyrinth and spread it round
That it devoured maidens, but I found
A starving cold and friendless beast, half blind.
It sensed my deadly purpose when I came
And caught within its throat a frightened breath,
Then bowed its head, subservient to death.
I clubbed it down and turned away in shame.

We did not linger on our voyage from Crete.
I drowned the memory in song and wine
And in my cups forgotten was the sign:
White sail to show success; black for defeat.
My father scanned the sea with nervousness.
Black was the sail – it seems he knew despair
And hurled himself to death. I, son and heir,
Have benefited from forgetfulness.

by D Shepherd

Forgetting

I've forgotten how it feels to be outrageously in love,
To be waiting by the phone for her to ring;
I've forgotten all the breathlessness of blushing adolescence
And the thrill of winter dancing into spring.
I remember reading Pushkin and the tinkling of the troika
As it sped on silent runners through the snow;
How I wish the troika's magic might convey me from my
    window
To the fields that I discarded long ago.

I'm forgetting – I'm forgetting simple facts that were so easy
For an infant to remember. I forget
What I did last Sunday evening, where I went to in the summer;
What it is that makes me wallow in regret.
As I shelter in my bedroom I hear footsteps on the staircase,
Or enthusiastic voices in the hall;
How I dread the day approaching when my children stand beside
    me
And their names are foreign words I can't recall.

Let it be that, when finality accords me blind affection
And my eyes forget the loves they used to know,
I shall slip into a slumber as a youthful troika takes me
Into blizzards of oblivion and snow.

by Frank McDonald

Cacophony

The Cocks of Kiseljak: A Ballad of the United Nations in Bosnia

The cocks that crowed in Kiseljak they woke a thousand men,
and, as each man turned in his sack and tried to sleep again,
he cursed the cocks of Kiseljak and wished them dole and pain.

Until, one dawn – Saint Martin's day, good saint of martial men -
these thousand curses soared aloft, floated a while and then
became, through holy alchemy, the feathers of the hen.

Look, where a thousand feathers spin above the little town
and form ten squads of ten by ten and each squad wheels around,
adopts the likeness of a hen and drifts towards the ground.

At once the crowing cocks observe these slick chicks from the skies.
Lewd passion swells their every nerve, it thrills their trembling thighs.
They gaze on each descending curve with wildly prurient eyes.

And when the insubstantial flock has floated to the ground
The noisy cocks of Kiseljak go to it with a bound,
eager to mount a fleshly back where no flesh can be found.

And in and out the feathers fly where cockerels vainly thrust
and feath'ry tail and gauzy thigh give way to ash and dust
until those roosters roll and lie castrated by their lust.

And now the town of Kiseljak, since that Saint Martin's morn,
knows only gentle, caponed cocks who whisper to the dawn
while soldiers slumber in the sack like pretty babes new-born.

by Ralph Rochester

The Bombardment

I'm dug into the earth, and curled up like a child
It's pouring with rain, but I'm drowning in fear
For the Big Guns are howling, and seething with rage
A crescendo of death as the barrage creeps near.
Louder! and Louder! shredding the night
The great guns are cursing and screaming with hate
The half-tracks are burning, the fuel dumps ignite,
In a grave called a foxhole a man waits his fate.
The bloodthirsty shrapnel is fleaming, and cloying
The shells, they are screeching, the mortars explode
The bombers are pounding our souls into dust
In the wet earth I bury myself like a toad.
Hour after hour, and each hour's a lifetime,
We're hammered, we're shattered, we're blasted apart
And the noise, ever louder, turns hard rock to jelly
As the screams of the dying explode in the heart.
In the bowels of the earth that is heaving and churning
An army is turning to stinking manure;
Pride, she is dead, but Chaos is shrieking
And Death, ever hungry, is howling for more.
I leap from my bed, from the sweat of my dreaming
I hear all the screaming, though now I am deaf.
I see all the faces, though my eyes are shattered
And I smell the destruction with my every breath.

by Alfred Peter Hollick

The Last Trump

Cathedral, temple, mosque and mission hall,
Each one denies the tenets of the rest
And claims its faith alone is best of all
And only through its gods can men be blessed.
The afterlife is at the central core
Of what the sects can offer: each sets out
What to expect when passing through death's door
As if it were well known and free from doubt.

It is remarkable to be so clear!
There's been no revenant come from the tomb
The secrets of the charnel house to share
And the procedures of the catacomb.
The huckster voices fill the atmosphere,
Accusing, angry, fearful, wise, absurd,
And make a dissonance in the world's ear
In which no single message can be heard.

It may be that some day the trump will sound
And on that day the living and the dead
Will hear, awestruck, the voice of God resound.
There'll be no doubt who speaks, nor what is said.

by D Shepherd

Spring Cleaning

The Admonition

When you spring-clean your heart, as soon you must,
Another's hopes therein to entertain,
Take care that not the smallest specks of dust,
Or atoms of my presence there remain.
For if he, whose you shall be then, can find
Those tell-tale traces of an earlier guest,
Your promises of love will be divined
As second-hand, and therefore second best.
So polish up your secrets, let them gleam
As new again in this admirer's eye,
Then may you both conspire to share a dream
Of truth, and innocent together lie.
Since love neglected often turns to hate,
By this, its myth you may perpetuate.

by Laurence Joyce

Spring Clean

They took your clothes at Oxfam, and your shoes,
The way you looked all folded in a sack,
Your 'Friday' ties, your old 'Columbo' mac,
The pink-striped shirt I took so long to choose.
Your wardrobe gapes, swept grimly clean of clues,
The shelves detergent-scrubbed from front to back
And rows of empty hangers on the rack
Now made redundant droop in silent queues.
Good friends and green narcissus shoots proclaimed
With sunny grace: the tidying time was due
And I must sweep and polish unashamed,
Embrace my single future, fresh and new.
But what can ever bleach bereavement's stain,
Dust dreams away, or disinfect my pain?

by Diana Newlands

Bibliophobia

Today I'm throwing out a thousand books,
Old Gorgon texts that turned my soul to stone;
I hate their pious, disapproving looks
That weighed my worthless life beside their own.
I cannot bear to see the sombre place
Where Dostoevsky rests alongside Gide,
Or where some Latin verse sits in disgrace
With student notes that I shall never read.
The room is loud with voices no one hears:
Spinoza, Plato, Kant and Schopenhauer;
I shall evict them, after all these years,
And free my captive conscience from their power.
My fruitless life – who knows? – might find a meaning
In this spring purge, this literary cleaning.

by Andrew Brison

One Spring Morning

With sunlit thoughts, she dusts the photograph
Depicting her late spouse – false teeth and all,
Replaces it above the sleeping hearth
Then moves on to the china in the hall.
Before long, all the house seems spick and span
Save for a cobwebbed wardrobe, so she flails
Her duster round its contents, making plans
To sell them at the local church hall sale.
Remembering there's the kitchen floor to mop
She turns, about to close the wardrobe door
When, from a greyed and fading tracksuit top,
A small address book tumbles to the floor.
She stares at it a while then looks inside
And finds out where he'd slept and how he'd lied.

by Richard Otto

Turning Out

She stood irresolute one winter's day
Stuck on a traffic crossing, half aware
That Spring quite suddenly was on the way,
New birth, new life, new stirring everywhere.

She doubled back and mercifully missed
A close encounter with a speeding car.
The driver waved an agitated fist.
She did not see. Her mind was all ajar.

She bought some snowdrops on the corner stall –
Small white tapers to light up the gloom –
And thought 'Tomorrow I'll spring-clean the hall,
And then I will attack the living room.'

But lurking at the bottom of her mind
She found intentions of a wilder kind.

by Angela Greenhill

Trespass

Out of Bounds

Scrumping apples, taking pheasants, parson's orchard, squire's grounds,
from the moment he could toddle he was always out of bounds.
Out of bounds was all his glory, breaking bounds was all his fun
from the first page of his story to the setting of his sun.

He who never told his triumphs, he who never showed his wounds,
worked and played and loved and hated, lived and perished out of bounds.
Midnight scuffles, reckless gambles, bitter struggles, headlong flights,
raddled virgins, shunted babies, slothful days and guilty nights.

He who never climbed a mountain, he who never rode to hounds
found the thrills and spills he wanted, and he found them out of bounds.
Bootleg gin and wayward women, moonshine whiskey, pretty boys,
laundered money all his stipend, dirty doings all his joys.

Lay him gently in his coffin, he'll be back to do the rounds.
Heaven's gates or hell's damnation, you can bet he'll break the bounds.
Out of bounds was all his glory, breaking bounds was all his fun
from the first page of his story to the setting of his sun.

by Ralph Rochester

The Snake's Song

There was a time when all of this was mine:
the earth, the grass, the white flowers and the trees,
the swelling roots, the green, embracing vine
weighed down with clustered fruit, and more than these,
the rocks that make black shadows every day,
the fields that run to where the sky begins,
the paths that move and twist and show the way
to everywhere. So what have been my sins?
What is the something wrong I must have done
to earn a punishment as harsh as this?
Those two are trespassing. God is the one
who licensed them to spoil my silent bliss.
He told them they may share this place with me.
We'll see. I have a plan. I'll hibernate.
As sure as apples redden on the tree,
they won't last long. And I know how to wait.

by Adèle Geras

A Curious Hobby

A Curious Hobby

Bug-hunters they were called; a canting term
That meant, in nineteenth-century public schools,
Amused derision, tolerant contempt
Of boys more drawn to nature than to games.
One such there was, described as 'uninspired'
By his headmaster, who abandoned school
To study medicine. Repelled by that,
He went to Cambridge, where his idle ways
Earned a divinity degree, but not a call.
And all the time the bugs and beetles grew
In cabinets of stacked mahogany.
At length his baffled father, who had friends,
Placed him as gentleman-companion
And naturalist aboard a survey ship
Bound for Cape Horn, and thence Galapagos.
He came back rich in samples, and much more:
The slow ferment of beetles, bugs and beaks
Worked on his mind until, against his will,
But sure as any Robespierre, he stirred up
A revolution that is echoing yet.

by Noel Petty

Harmless Fun

I like to fondle strangers that I meet:
Young women, soft and warm and not too thin,
On buses, at the pictures, in the park.
I like to feel my skin against their flesh.

It's not that I am trying to attract,
Or desperately looking for romance;
Just curious to see how they respond,
And whether they are wearing any tights.

You'd be surprised the fuss some of them make.
I could have many hobbies ten times worse:
Collect antiques, breed ferrets or bake bread,
Write poetry and bore the world with rhymes.

So come on, ladies, make me thrilled to bits,
And let me get my hands upon your knees.

by Richard Charles

The Solicitor

Midsummer on the steamy streets of town
Where women fluttered by in filmy scraps
Of muslin, silk and such, while men perspired
In standard two-piece suits and shirts and ties.
And he conformed; or so it seemed to those
Who came and sought his sound advice on wills,
Divorce, or disputes over land. Only
He knew that, underneath his sober grey
Attire, his shaven legs were clad in sleek,
Expensive hose and black satin panties
Graced his trim behind. At weekends, freed from
Work's restraints, made-up, golden wig in place,
He dressed in women's clothes and hung around
High-class hotels to look for lonely men.
Some drinks, sweet talk about his looks, the way
He moved, fulfilled his need. Maybe a kiss,
Then Cinderella-like he vanished in
The night, while in the bar the stranger cursed
His luck. And there he was, across the desk,
Quite unaware he's with the one he lost.

by Maureen A Jeffs

Harmony

Resolution

I'm not going to write about music
And certainly not about peace;
I choke with non-love for that horrible dove
That Picasso once drew when especially blue
And would gladly assist its decease.

I hate the avuncular vicar
Who's sure that all humans are nice;
His tuneless guitar and clap-happy choir
Singing newly-purged hymns make me reach for the Pimms
And dream of unspeakable vice.

Don't give me the Yogic insistence
On balance between the extremes;
The bores who advise that one must compromise
I would happily boil in their own social oil,
Ignoring their tedious screams.

To hell with the thought of creating
A bland and harmonious whole;
The pleasures of strife bring zest to my life . . .
Perhaps I was meant to be full of dissent.
The thought brings strange peace to my soul.

by Alison Prince

Parfaite Harmonie

The gentle academic folk
Were slumbering in their chairs
When distant voices came and broke
Upon their ears, and on the stairs
A step was heard; a voice declared:
"I deconstruct, I look at words,
I roust them out, I get them aired,
I turn them into little birds,
They fly about, they loop the loop,
The alphabet becomes a soup.

"I show the harm in harmony,
The sham in our champagne.
I see the ire in irony,
The moon in things mundane.
I love the mar in marriages,
The end of burn is urn;
The first part of miscarriages
Is rarely *his* concern.
Nothing is really what it seems,
Except, perhaps, in people's dreams."

The gentle academic folk
Stopped listening, and were bored,
Until the voice no longer spoke,
And harmony was restored.

by Bill Philips

The Lyre

The people are quelled when they hide from a raid
of bombs that destroy, though they mean to degrade.
These targets and missiles will both disappear
when daylight arrives and the skies are all clear.

Then tractors tow bundles of grannies and bags,
with daughters well hidden from rapists by rags.
The women are weeping away from it all,
whilst bullets tap tunes through the men by the wall.

The tellies are telling us just who to blame,
whilst men in grey suits are all saying the same
words for just wars, which they use to deceive,
since words, which are true, we might just not believe.

The people are streaming; the pilots still fly;
the broken are screaming; the leaders still lie.
The discords of war are composed for a choir
of devils to sing to the tunes of a liar.

by Mick Humphreys

Summer Follies

Little Follies

Follies Gothic, follies Grecian
Built to gratify a whim,
Smiling down at parkland ha-has
From their perch aloof and trim
Or set serenely near the lakeside
With waterlilies at their feet,
A charming architectural nonsense
To make the scheme of things complete.
Summers come and summers vanish,
Cold winds chill their sun-warmed stone,
Chestnuts tumble – horse and Spanish -
Little follies dream alone,
Aliens in the park or garden,
Symbols of another age,
Small intruders begging pardon
For invading such a stage.
More cherished than their grander cousins
I think that they are haunted still
By little footsteps in their dozens
And childish laughter sweet and shrill.

by Angela Greenhill

Summer Follies

Was it yesterday we hurried to make castles by a bay
and the waves ignored our laughter, sweeping everything away?
All the flurries of excitement, all our shyness, every tear,
all were washed away forever, every summer, every year?
In those sudden summer downpours when our skin was pink
 with rain
and our lips felt loveless kisses we would never taste again,
did we realise such follies would just melt away as snow,
that the wine that we were drinking was the best we'd ever
 know?
On a bridge above a railway track we watched a train approach
and its fetid breath around us bore excitement we could touch;
how we laughed with blackened faces as the wagons thundered
 past,
never knowing that the silence that rushed after them would last.
Is it possible that somewhere all those follies linger on,
and that children play in secret every evening, every dawn?
Are there pathways to an innocence, immune from adult rage?
Is it possible to glimpse them from the windowsill of age?
We can hear them if we listen, when our night is lush with stars;
we can hear them, faint and distant, through the thunder of our
 years.
As we close our bedroom window they invite us to go back
but our steps are far too weary to retrace that youthful track.

by Frank McDonald

Summer Song

The sun is full of swallows,
The sky is baby blue,
The bees are drunk on nectar
And the grass is wet with dew.
The seagulls and the sea breeze
Are hung above the town,
And I'm in love with the bicycle girl
Who's young and blonde and brown.

Amongst the ripe tomatoes
A plane bisects the sky,
And up and down the fragrant street
The sweaty prams go by.
A ginger cat is swinging
Lopsided in a tree,
And I'm in love with the bicycle girl
Who's wild and fresh and free.

by David Hill

Summer Follies

The friend upon the wall was now her foe:
That shiny, blank, cold-hearted square whose gaze
She could not meet for fear it would expose
Time's measured lines that nothing could erase.

The doorbell's strident call drew her away,
And there he stood – an object of desire -
A man who'd come because she sought advice
On gardens and design. A man for hire.

She watched him from her window as he worked,
Stripped naked to the waist, to recreate
Some beauty from the years of past neglect.
Her fallow bed lay ready for a mate.

Each day at noon she called him to the door
To tempt him with a snack, some tasty treat;
Until the day he took her in his arms,
Caressed her, and they both forgot to eat.

They made love in the kitchen, in the hall,
Alfresco, under stars out on the lawn.
She, like the garden, flowered at his touch;
She woke each day and felt she was reborn.

The Indian summer of her heart burnt bright;
And though she knew some thought she was unwise,
The mirror now confirmed she was alive,
Reflecting back the pleasure in her eyes.

by Maureen A Jeffs

Lips That Lie

Lips that Lie

They dipped their fingers in the dish
While one shared out the bread,
Then, hearing that stark work, 'Betray',
"Lord, is it I?" they said.

One figure on a couch reclined
(He kept the common purse),
The selfsame question of his friends
His lips, too, did rehearse.

It was a careless tone of voice,
Uttered in feigned surprise
By one who, in the world of men,
Sat easy in disguise.

But this was not just any meal
Of simple bread and wine,
Nor was it any upper room
For them that came to dine.

And he who lay and lolled and laughed,
"Good master, is it I?"
Glanced up but could not meet the gaze
Of him who could not lie.

Then silently he let fall down
The blest and broken bread
And heard, as though a long way off,
"This have your own lips said."

by Jack Carrigan

Clear Blue Water

They met in the hotel corridor, in the heat-trapped, shuttered gloom,
And he rested his hands on her sun-touched hips as they wandered back to their room.
"How were your castles and churches?" she asked; "I've been in the sea.
I love that sea, and you, my love, love ruins more than me."

She peeled away her swimming things and threw them to dry on the sill,
And he kissed her mouth and her chuckling throat and the room was suddenly chill,
For he tasted the evening cool of her skin and lips that were touched by wine,
But he tasted no salt on her golden neck, no ocean-gilded brine.

Stale fears revived as he contrived to twist her lie to the true,
And dry and uncouth came the dusty truth he knew or thought that he knew:
That she could take a passing love to lighten a solitary day,
Like a child who breaks a precious thing then laughs and wanders away.

"I swam by the river's mouth," she said, "where the trees come down to the shore,
And the water's sweet a long way out, a hundred yards or more.
You can drink the waves; tomorrow, please come, your ruins will still be there."
"Tomorrow we'll swim in the sea," he said, and buried his smile in her hair.

by Nick Syrett

Lip Service

If Cupid did not give you bows,
do not despair, for there are ways
to beat genetics and disclose
a vibrant you, evoking praise

from lovers who will kiss if they
are fooled enough. I bid you cheat.
Go find a surgeon who will play
a game that makes you more complete.

For there are those with scalpels sharp
and sculptural skills beyond our ken
who beautify where others carp
and help you lure seductive men.

Love only comes to those who try.
Submerge your pride, invest your all
and learn through joy that lips that lie
are better than no lips at all.

by Patricia V Dawson

Psalm

Magnificat

All glory to our modern race
Whose genius can conquer space,
Whose scientists have found the key
To deconstruct biology
And diligently peel away
The secrets of our DNA.

For unpolluted air we yearn,
Green unspoilt earth our main concern.
Wise family planning we uphold
And build smart homes to house the old.
Our children's whims we do not thwart
And never chase the fox for sport.

We cannot follow ancient creeds
But bend the rules to suit our needs.
New gods we worship, fitness, health,
And schemes that bring us instant wealth,
And football players, TV stars,
Computers and expensive cars.

For all the many thousand ways
We have progressed, ourselves we praise;
And yet instead of promised bliss
We stare into a great abyss.
What are those joys for which we long?
Can we perhaps have got it wrong?

by O Smith

Cantate Domino

Let's sing a new song to the Lord,
The sort that they love to record -
That grabs people's hearts,
Goes straight to the charts
And gets us a Grammy award.

Let's sing of miraculous grace
And love for the whole human race,
With bags of salvation
And amplification
On vocals and keyboards and bass.

Let's sing about heaven, and then
Let's sing it all over again
As we watch the dosh flow
And the interest grow
For ever and ever. Amen.

by Joan Butler

The Fall

A Life

Fell off a bike when I was three,
Bashed my head and skinned my knee,
Fell out with Mum when I was ten
And never quite fell in again,
Fell for a guy with a dazzling smile
And the cut-throat charm of a crocodile,
Fell pregnant and produced a son
Who's never honestly been much fun,
Fell out of love and into debt
From which I've not recovered yet,
Fell out of work and out of favour,
Life has steadily lost its flavour.

Write a note and end it all.
"Stranger, I jumped. I did not fall."

by Alison Prince

The Fall of a Queen

Ah, little lady on a swing,
Enjoying games that please a king,
Dream, dream your dreams in summer air,
His is a voice you should not hear.
Your laughter rings around his court
Down past the lawns of regal sport,
With hawk in hand he passes by,
Loves you already with his eye.

What fancies fill that foolish head
When you are warm in Henry's bed?
You think you'll bend him to your will,
That beauty has the power to kill,
But on the streets they call you whore;
See, Henry goes to hunt once more,
Seeking another girlish face,
Another queen to take your place.

Poor princess of the fragrant breath
A son means life, a daughter death,
And all your winning wiles in bed
Will not protect that lovely head.
One last request he will accord -
No blunted axe but shining sword
Will cut your neck, sweet Anne Boleyn.
This was a game you could not win.

by Frank McDonald

THE FALL

How Despised are the Fallen

He fell, they said, from an enormous height,
Unable to sustain his power of flight,
Dashed to the ground, a heap of broken bones
And crumpled wings. In reverential tones
At first they spoke of him, a tragedy,
They said, for one so innocent and free.

Then they saw the streaks of melted wax
That glistened in the feathers' finest cracks,
And wondered what had happened to bring down
This one who yearned to wear the winner's crown.
High flier, yes, but wasn't it his fault
For taking needless risks and getting caught?

Fired with ambition many a young man
Has tried to reach the top, work out his plan
To beat the odds. How wonderful, we say,
Look at him now, he's really got away,
Leading the field, or standing high above
Competitors, this is success we love.

But let him fall, for sticking out his neck,
Or climbing up too fast – we see the wreck,
And, wincing at the sight, avert our eyes.
As onlookers, forever hindsight wise,
We mutter that he never seemed to learn.
Those who fly too high will always burn.

by Katie Mallett

Dalliance

Madrigal

Fair Phyllis was a shepherdess and Corydon her swain.
They sported in the woodland while her sheep grazed in the
   plain,
For in those days the sheep were always well-behaved and neat,
A feature of the landscape rather than a source of meat.
Thus shepherdesses were quite free to range those sylvan scenes,
And evidently rustic swains were blessed with private means,
For Corydon would pipe all day, and tuneful birds would sing,
And nymphs would turn up now and then to foot it in a ring.
But mostly Phyllis feigned escape, and Corydon would follow
Until they stumbled quite by chance into some secret hollow.
The sun shone all the time, and summer never left the stage.
The fruit was permanently ripe. It was a Golden Age.

Two thousand years roll by until we reach the present day,
And Corydon and Phyllis now have little time to play.
For him, a banker, time is worth two hundred pounds an hour,
While she, a media exec, has caught a whiff of power.
He labours fourteen hours a day, somewhere in Lombard Street,
And weekends find him fawning in some hospitality suite.
She's a martyr to her mobile, the servant that dictates,
And every moment spare will see her working out with weights.
But both of them are on the web, and so these lovers two
Can take a frenzied break to send virtual billet doux,
Telling – in haste – how much by each the other is adored.
Thus, by the grace of e-mail, is the Golden Age restored.

by Noel Petty

Dalliance

Do not dream, foolish heart, this is more than mere fancy –
this amorous trifle's a flash in the pan –
a brief peccadillo to counteract boredom
of dutiful marriage to one dreary man.

Never think, for a moment, this passing attraction
might kindle some spark of romantic desire,
his smile may be warm and his blood even hotter
but lust fuels the flames of his thrill-hungry fire.

He is charming, attentive, a wonderful lover
(but never too serious), eager to please
while the mood is light-hearted, giddy with kisses,
and sex is a sport played with blind referees.

You're just a notch on his belt, a moment's amusement,
a pleasant diversion, a hobby he's found
engaging, at least while the game is still novel,
this scoring of goals on another guy's ground.

If you must dip a toe in the bright pool of passion,
don't be tempted to dive – it's a whim, nothing more -
a pound to a penny the water runs shallow
so best keep the other foot firm on the floor.

by J M Harvey

Our Days of Dalliance

Remember, remember the wealth that we squandered,
the posies of promises withered away;
O why did we linger on baubles and trifles,
believing our boyhood ambitions would stay?
Remember when springtime was verdant before us,
when life was eternal and love was our dream,
when students we stood on the steps of our college
and called on our Muse to make pleasure the theme.
We dallied too long in those languorous summers,
enthralled by the playthings of ignorant youth,
with never a thought for the long winter evenings
when feeble old fingers would fumble for truth.
But God, it was good to be flippant and foolish,
to laugh at sagacity, mock the austere,
to bask in abundance of slow-moving minutes,
and welcome the dawn of another new year.
Could not the fair nymphs of a lighter existence
besprinkle our moments with yesterday's fun,
and whisper in tones that would make us believe them
that there is still time to fly up to the sun

by Frank McDonald

Loitering with Intent

Quite talented, my teachers said,
 But doesn't seem to stick at things,
Fails to understand the gain
 That perseverance brings;
It's true I've never felt the need
 To graft along through life,
Not for me the crushing millstone
 Of the dedicated life,
Round the fringes of existence
 I have dawdled time away,
Canoodled, flirted, trifled
 Through each undemanding day;
Wayward as the autumn leaves
 That frisk along the street
On paths that lead to nowhere
 I have set my dragging feet,
While on roads unfit for loitering
 Humanity speeds by,
Trapped in mad contention
 Where to linger is to die;
Our journey's end is certain
 Take whatever route we may,
But at least I claim the option
 To dally on the way.

by Philip A Nicholson

In Praise of Slough

Apology from Above

Mid the heavenly hosts in eternal procession,
Neath pillars and porticoes splendidly proud,
Sir John, with his halo and hangdog expression,
Sits sipping Typhoo on a marshmallow cloud.

"I'm sorry," he pleads, "if in youth I offended
The township and Godfearing people of Slough.
My unkindly aspersions had best be amended:
You're surely no worse than the rest of them now.

Since the Windsors and Weybridges, once so delightful,
With teashops and taverns and meadows beyond,
Have been turned in a trice into equally frightful
Facsimile forms of your Slough of Despond.

Their High Streets, like yours, have that mind-numbing sameness.
Where Natwests and Kwik-fits and Tescos abound.
Their doorways awash with identikit, shameless,
Brash mendicant youths (with a well-nourished hound).

So cheer up, old Slough! You were first of the many!
But sweet recollections embarrass me now;
For the chocs of my childhood I bought for a penny,
Were made by the Mars Corporation – in *Slough!*

O Bounty! O Milky Way! O my Malteser!
I long for you now mid these perishing stars.
What comfort you'd bring to a grumpy old geezer
(Who's sick of ambrosia). Oh for a Mars!"

by J M Turner

In Praise of Slough

Now if a pleasant Thames-side stroll
That ends in free verse rigmarole,
Can be portrayed as poetry
In honour of the TUC;
Then poetry in praise of Slough
Might further wanderings allow,
To suit the philosophic state
Affected by a Laureate.

Once Laureates could rhyme and scan,
The last of them was Betjeman,
Who wrote of girls on tennis courts
And gave a hint of darker thoughts;
And now with expectation gone,
Those friendly bombs he called upon,
Its citizens may come to see,
Raised Slough to immortality.

by Robert Marks

Slough Old and New

Old Slough, that once was Upton's field
and where the infant Herschel's eyes
first blinked up at the starry skies
enchanted by their silver yield;
where stage-coach horses once clip-clopped
along the western way to Bath
and now great lorries blast a path
tanking up where coaches stopped -

Old rubbish dump of the Great War
then beacon light of the Depression,
turning the tables on recession
and rising stronger than before,
you have good cause for civic pride,
honour your Borough and enjoy it,
Betjebombs cannot destroy it
nor mar your lovely countryside.

Stoke Poges still remembers Gray,
a ghostly curfew tolls for him
and as the winter light grows dim
his shadow flits along the way
to old St. Lawrence Church maybe
where, unquiet shade with troubled mind,
may he compose for human kind
some strange millennial elegy?

by Angela Greenhill

Money

Crisis

Beneath the city's heedless blare
Where daylight's beams have never shone
Lie deep the silent caverns, where
The gold of nations slumbers on.

A High Official breaks the hush,
A clutch of master keys in hand.
A whispered word; his minions rush
To execute his tense command.

Performing to a practised plan
They wheel a dozen bars or more
Out of the cage marked *Pakistan*
Into the one marked *Ecuador*.

The High Official rolls his eyes,
His colour now recovering.
"The world is safe once more," he sighs,
"But God! it was a close-run thing."

by Noel Petty

Money

I had a dream and in it I
Fell screaming from a Grecian sky,
Impacting on the ocean's skin
And fifty fathoms plummetting.
And on the mossy, soft sea-bed
I came upon a corpse who said,
"My name is Xerxes. I am he
Who tried to castigate the sea.
My friends are those who were too rich -
Cyrus, Phlebas and other such.
There's Morgan here, and Maxwell, too.
We are a melancholy crew."
He, saying this, began to weep
As sea-snakes from his eyes did creep.
I looked in Maxwell's mouth and saw
A lurking crab with sharpened claw
That snapped above and snapped beneath,
Worrying at his gold-capped teeth.
Those ghostly death-mates gathered round,
All gibbering with bat-like sound,
All holding out their hands in grief
And cursing their lost coins. In brief,
It haunted them, now they were dead.
I woke, perspiring, on my bed.

by Janice Novaya

The Money Tree: a Fable

"Stay," called the wind to the traveller,
"While the rain from my soft warm sky,
Fills lake and dene
Till earth is green";
But the traveller hurried by.
"I need no dreams
Of crystal streams
For I travel where riches lie."

"Stay," called the sun to the traveller,
"I will ripen the tall palm tree,
And you may eat
Fruit soft and sweet";
But the traveller would not see.
"I hear, I think,
The magic clink
Of the fruit of the money tree."

They called again to the traveller
On the wild desert road he chose;
But all they found
Was thirsty ground
With lost travellers' bones in rows.
No soil, no sand,
Just flint-hard land
Where they say the money tree grows.

by Ted Giles

Wednesday

The Colour of Wednesday

Come, my love, and search for meaning
In the colours of the days
While the blades and leaves are greening,
Soil's forsaking idle ways.
Thursday's purple long receded,
Friday's yellow out of sight,
Saturday no longer needed
With its image of pure white,
Sunday's gold and Monday's crimson,
Tuesday's orange, passed away;
What's in Wednesday to sing hymns on?
What's the colour of today?

Wednesday's brown, the bare earth's colour,
Soon for covering with green.
What, you ask me, could be duller?
Better to be never seen.
Rather let our gaze entwining
Meet brown eyes, as deep as day,
Each to each in love inclining,
Soft brown hair in disarray.
Till our skin is browner, firmer,
Summer sand or polished wood;
Hold me tight, my love, and murmur,
Wednesday's honest brown is *good*.

by Paul Griffin

Euro-Wash

I wash my wife on Wednesday.
I often wonder why.
I think it's that: till Saturday
Her hair has time to dry.

Oh! Wednesday! Oh! Wednesday!
The middle of the week.
I wash my wife on Wednesday
And kiss her steamy cheeks!

I fill the tub right to the brim,
Likewise a glass of brandy:
So when it's time to push her in
I'm feeling rather handy.

Oh Wednesday! Oh Wednesday!
Mitten in der Woche.
I wash my wife on Wednesday,
Ordentlich and proper.

Her slippery extremities
My foamy fingers fumble,
Each protuberance and crevice
Endures my rumble-tumble.

Oh! Wednesday! Oh! Wednesday!
En milieu de semaine.
I wash my wife on Wednesday
Encore! Once more! Again!

by Colonel G H Peebles

Wednesday

That evening I travelled, as always,
Unsuspecting what fate had supplied,
Or was that a vague premonition
As I gazed at the darkness outside?

Speak of love to your dear ones and always
Give them cause to remember with pride
All the things you accomplished together.
Ask forgiveness for times when you lied.

The front door was open, as always,
But where was the welcome inside?
Instead of his smile there was silence
On that Wednesday in March when he died.

by Maureen Brampton

Last Love

In Heaven's Despite

The winter was cold, you were thirty years old,
And I was a twelve-year-old boy.
And we walked in the rain, and you bandaged my pain,
And you taught me the meaning of joy.

We were love, we were wild, made a miracle child,
Walked on air, set the night-time aglow.
When our daughter was born, you were bleeding and torn,
And you blamed me, you blamed me, I know.

I sent her a note and a poem I wrote
On a sailboat with gossamer sails.
You wanted a son, so you gave her a gun
And a collar of leather and nails.

She had to leave home, so she lived on her own
For as long as she wanted to live.
The night that she hanged, the telephone rang.
She said, "Mummy, I'm sorry. Forgive."

You stayed supple and thin, you put oil on your skin,
You still look good by soft candlelight.
And the boys come to call, and you sleep with them all,
And they only stay, ever, one night.

It's too late now to care, so I help with your hair,
And I clean up the things that you spill.
And I still can't forget your love when we met,
And I don't think I ever quite will.

by Richard Charles

Last Love

Never have I once pretended
To be your only, first or best,
Uniquely loved, seduced, befriended . . .
But spare me details of the rest,
Of lovers conquered, unrequited,
Torrid, frigid, dark or blonde,
As if you think I'd be excited
To hear of past loves, fast or fond.

Childhood sweethearts, Soho tarts
And other men's frustrated wives;
Bodies, trophies, vanquished hearts -
Your boasts and memories haunt our lives
No more. The green-eyed monster's dead
With one premeditated blast.
A single bullet to your head.
I'm not your latest, but your last.

by Catherine Dampier

Eloïse and Abelard: A Last Love

For them it was last love: it left no hope
For him or her; and so this sad affair
Inspired the rhymes of poets everywhere
And, best of all, a masterpiece by Pope.

Suppose it hadn't ended in that way.
Suppose that it had run its natural course:
A wedding, then young children, then divorce,
A pattern that seems usual today.

Kids in bewilderment, despair or, worse,
Rejected and emotionally berserk –
A footnote in a book on social work
But unfit matter for romantic verse.

by Derek Muncey

London

London

There is another map, instead
Of this torn, dog-eared A–Z;
An overlay of chance, loose ends,
With shades of lovers, names of friends;
Streets where each paving stone brings back
Cold tear-stained nights when all looked black;
The corner of which plane-strewn square
Witnessed the end of an affair,
Or gardens where love's blossoming
Was bright, more green than any Spring.

No printed index gives it sense
Or recognises difference.
This is a map whose nerve ends go
Through stuccoed, dream-like Pimlico,
A map of heart-lines, not revealed
In idle search for Bunhill Fields,
An inner gazetteer, each name
Marked with a plaque for loss, or blame;
Unguided, guarded to the last,
The private London of the past.

by D A Prince

The Backwoodsman

When a man is tired of London he is tired of life.

Samuel Johnson

Many a weekend I spent with Keats
In my digs high above the Lambeth streets;
And for my recreation ran
Through Lambeth Walk with Kubla Khan;
And in the crowds along Whitehall
I saw the shade of Bernard Shaw,
The greatest writer of his time.
(He told us so time after time.)

Then came that day at Waterloo,
A crowd too many, and I knew
That Doctor Johnson got it wrong -
That life could sing a sweeter song.
I heard the call of the field-green sea,
Of the sea-green fields that were home to me.
I traded The Strand for a Dartmoor track,
Left London behind, and never went back.

by Edward Murch

The Synoptic Londoner

Holmes fidgets in his lodgings but his mind is far away,
Far down the Thames where life is cheap and villainy holds sway,
Where the wharf rat smuggles opium and the cutpurse whets his knife,
Where darkness masks the violent deed and robbery is rife.
Out East, beyond the City, there's a capital of crime
Whose felony and evil match the river's tidal slime.
No copper can walk safely there, no writ of law avail,
But hardened villains curse their luck when Holmes is on the trail.

Holmes throws his half-read paper down; his eyes are eagle-keen.
It's Holmes the great detective now, the reasoning machine,
Who, dressed for dirty work afoot and taciturn of speech,
Will hail a passing hansom cab and head for Limehouse Reach.
There, passing as a beggar or a surly, whiskered groom
He'll be the Nemesis of rogues, the scofflaw's certain doom;
The Great Wen has its secrets, its abodes of hidden shame,
But Holmes sees all and knows all: he's the master of the game.

by Iain Colley

Leaving Home

He'd left the gentle village, seeking fame
In London, where the streets were paved with gold,
And chances to acquire a golden name
Fell from the sky like dew (so he was told).
The city's prospect, after many a day,
Appalled his senses. Vulgarness defaced
The ancient walls with anger and dismay;
And all seemed dirt and mindlessness and waste.
Yet, as he stood on Ludgate Hill, below
The vision raised his buoyant hopes again,
As night and winter covered all in snow,
Hiding the gross minutiae of men.
Down to the creeping river where the light
Of roisterous inns and magic theatres beamed,
He stared for miles and wondered at the sight,
Warmed by the fire of futures he had dreamed.
He had done little yet. This was the place.
In this quick forge and printing house of fame,
He'd brood and bustle and devoutly chase
The insubstantial glory of a name.
This was the place and time to be alive.
The lad was Shakespeare, 1585.

by Colin Pearson

Foreign Parts

Foreign Parts

Once foreign parts were far away
And foreigners were there to stay,
And England had an empire yet
On which the sun declined to set;
Asylum meant the funny farm
And nationalism was no harm,
The monarchy was heaven sent
And laws were made by parliament.

Now England has an open door
And foreign parts are far no more,
With patriotic views forbidden
And laws of England overridden;
Instead we have correctness, cant,
Pretensions to be tolerant,
A refuge for the refugee
And anti-racist industry:
Indulgences that coalesce
To bring an end to foreignness.

by Robert Marks

African Evening, with Bats

We drink on the veranda in the glow
of humid dusk, now that the tropic glare
is fading in a flame-tree flush below
the sculpted greyness of the hills. Down where
an evening breeze will soon draw breath and stir
spiced scent from moonflowers, nervously we watch
etched branches cast their loads, leaf ghosts that whirr
across the valley. Faultlessly they catch
ascending currents. What is there to fear?
The timed perfection of the phalanx breaks;
some individuals, squealing, swoop too near
to superstition, fall as flickering flakes
in a black blizzard. We are fazed by flight,
clutch emptied glasses ringing with their cries.
Sieving the air for gnats, they turn to night.
The spell unwinds. We toast their mysteries.

by Alanna Blake

Hadrian's Wall

Reluctant daybreak blends with the noon's dull grey
As heavy clouds bear low
From the Northern hills where unknown spirits stray
And unseen terrors grow.

We, shivering soldiers from the forts, slow creep
And trudge the friendless wall,
Our fingers blue; scant is the watch we keep
As the flakes begin to fall.

Where are the small dark patient men who wait
For the thin drawn line to fray?
Does the forest hide them a few short yards from the gate
Or a hundred miles away?

Ye gods! How this dreary cheerless land appals
As the weary hours drag slow.
Before we sleep we mark on the dripping walls
How many days to go.

We dream of a sparkling sun on Southern seas,
The fragrance of the pine
And the fruitful slopes where grow the olive trees
And the purple laden vine,
Then wake to the biting Northern winds that freeze
This thin drawn line.

by W H Jarvis

Sphakian Hill, West Crete

There's something sad about a barren hill,
Naked and grey, denied the primal right
Enshrined in Mother Earth yearly to fill
Her lap with coloured patterns to delight
Both man and beast. No goats can gather here
Tinkling disordered lives, no lizards lie
In crafty cracks, no pulsing rabbits fear
The predator who plummets from the sky.
Give it a tree, just one, and let the mind
Imagine all the life contained in that:
The birds who hide, perhaps a sheep behind
Or shepherd slumped beneath a broad-brimmed hat.
Then close your eyes and think what might have been
And watch the actors shift that barren scene.

by D E Poole

Index of Poems

Admonition, The · Laurence Joyce 112
African Evening, with Bats · Alanna Blake 158
Afternoon Tea – 1917 · Brian Mitchell 36
Alzheimer's · Norman Bissett 51
Apology from Above · J M Turner 141
Aqua Viva · Fergus Gwynplaine MacIntyre 45
At Sundowning · Griselda Scott 24
Backwoodsman, The · Edward Murch 154
Beginning of Bliss? · Rannoch Melville Russell 55
Bibliophobia · Andrew Brison 114
Bibliophrolic · Joan Butler 67
Bliss is an Empty Room · Angela Greenhill 54
Bliss? · O Smith 53
Bombardment, The · Alfred Peter Hollick 110
Bring me my Tactical Nuclear Missile Launcher · Richard Charles 97
Brutus · D Shepherd 12
Cantate Domino · Joan Butler 133
Case for the Defence · Noel Petty 59
Cat · Prue Sheldon 50
Choirboys · Paul Griffin 83
Clear Blue Water · Nick Syrett 130
Cocks of Kiseljak: A Ballad of the United Nations in Bosnia, The · Ralph Richardson 109
Colour of Wednesday, The · Paul Griffin 147
Colour of Your Eyes, The · Richard Charles 105
Company · Jon Sayers 92
Crisis · Noel Petty 144
Curious Hobby, A · Noel Petty 119
Dalliance · J M Harvey 138
Dante's Legacy · Noel Petty 102
Das Brandopfer · Richard Charles 17
Dejeuner des Canotiers · Alanna Blake 96
Delius Myth · Joan Butler 94
Diana Revestita · Frank McDonald 35
Dispossessed, The · John Lord 23
Eager Heart, The · Philip A Nicholson 91
Elegy for Choirboys · O Smith 82

INDEX

Eloïse and Abelard: A Last Love · Derek Muncey 152
Englishman Abroad · Philip A Nicholson 26
Euro-Wash · Colonel G H Peebles 148
Evensong at Ely · Maureen A Jeffs 84
Face Below, The · Fiona Pitt-Kethley 57
Fall of a Queen, The · Frank McDonald 135
Father · Paul Griffin 34
Feeding of the Terrier · Noel Petty 14
Fig Leaves Forever · Mick Humphreys 39
Figs · Alison Prince 38
Figs · Fiona Pitt-Kethley 41
Fin de Siècle · Barbara Daniels 29
Fin de Siècle · Bill Greenwell 30
Fin de Siècle · Frank McDonald 27
First Passion · Terence Reid 87
Fish · John Lord 73
Fish-Eye · Alison Prince 72
Foreign Parts · Robert Marks 157
Forgetting · Frank McDonald 108
Fowler Revisited · Alanna Blake 40
Frailty? · Isabel Vincent 52
Frolic · D Shepherd 68
Frolic · John Wedge 70
Game · Giles de la Bédoyère 4
Hadrian's Wall · W H Jarvis 159
Harmless Fun · Richard Charles 120
Home is where the Shit is · Francis Mullen 7
How Despised are the Fallen · Katie Mallett 136
Hunt for Immortality, A · D Shepherd 49
I Need no Shadow Whispering in my Ear · Noel Petty 66
If I Tell You · Martin Piper 101
In Heaven's Despite · Richard Charles 150
In Praise of Plumpness · John Kerkhoven 54
In Praise of Slough · Robert Marks 142
Journey, A · Christine Whittemore 18
Kith and Kin · Laurence Joyce 76
Last Love · Catherine Dampier 151
Last Trump, The · D Shepherd 111
Leaving Home · Colin Pearson 156
Life, A · Alison Prince 134

INDEX

Lip Service · Patricia V
    Dawson 131
Lips that Lie · Jack Carrigan
    129
Little Follies · Angela
    Greenhill 125
Loitering with Intent · Philip
    A Nicholson 140
London · D A Prince 153
Long and the Short, The ·
    Philip A Nicholson 62
Losing Her · Richard Charles
    75
Loss · Alison Prince 104
Love's Treachery · Griselda
    Scott 9
Lyre, The · Mick Humphreys
    124
Madrigal · Noel Petty 137
Magnificat · O Smith 132
Mermaid · Laurence Joyce 43
Mirrors and Windows ·
    Stephen Constable 15
Money · Janice Novaya 145
Money Tree: A Fable, The ·
    Ted Giles 146
Muse of Silence, The · Caspian
    Richards 79
Mutuality · Philip A Nicholson
    32
My Heart Leaps Up · Ted
    Giles 90
Naming Passion · J M Harvey
    86
New Intake, The · M
Hammerton 60
Oblivion for the Grieving ·
    Ted Giles 106
Of Love Returned · Frank
    McDonald 103
One Spring Morning ·
    Richard Otto 115
Ottery St Mary · Vincent L
    Smith 47
Our Days of Dalliance · Frank
    McDonald 139
Out of Bounds · Ralph
    Rochester 117
Parfaite Harmonie · Bill Philips
    123
Party's Over Now, The ·
    Pamela Martin 80
Quarry · Barbara Daniels 48
Rebuilding · D A Prince 98
Reelin' Hame · Brian Mitchell
    25
Resolution · Alison Prince
    122
'Ripeness is All' · O Smith 65
Rubenesque · D A Prince 63
Scientist, The · Noel Petty 89
Sleet Street · C B Owen 13
Slough Old and New · Angela
    Greenhill 143
Snake's Song, The · Adèle
    Geras 118
Social Sandwich · Griselda
    Scott 37
Solicitor, The · Maureen A
    Jeffs 121

INDEX

Song of Innocence · Richard Charles 81
Spare Parts · D Shepherd 99
Sphakian Hill, West Crete · D E Poole 160
Spring Clean · Diana Newlands 113
Stalker, The · Alison Mortimer 22
Stalker, The · David Poole 19
Stalking · D A Prince 21
Star Gazing · Mick Humphreys 100
Still Frolicking After All These Years · Katie Mallett 69
Story of the Hammer and the Nail, The · Jonathan Pool 85
Stranded · Richard Charles 77
Sugar Daddy – A Warning · Isabel Vincent 33
Suicide Note · Philip A Nicholson 20
Summer Follies · Frank McDonald 126
Summer Follies · Maureen A Jeffs 128
Summer Song · David Hill 127
Sweet Talk · Richard Charles 31
Synoptic Londoner, The · Iain Colley 155
Thé Dansant, J M Harvey 28
Theseus · D Shepherd 107
"This Area is Reserved for the Wildlife" · D A Prince 1
To A Goldfish · O Smith 71
Traitor, The · Alison Prince 11
Trout Tickling · Mary Holtby 74
Truly, Madly and Deeply · Robert Jules Vincent 46
Turning Out · Angela Greenhill 116
Two Faced · Jane Edmond 16
Two-faced Streets · Jenny Proom 58
Undercurrent, The · Noel Petty 6
Unfinished Business · Robert Jules Vincent 56
Virtue? A Fig · Jane Falloon 42
Visit, A · Noel Petty 78
Wednesday · Maureen Brampton 149
Wild Life · Paul Griffin 2
Wild Life · D A Prince 1
Wings and the Wake, The · David Rogers 88
Ye shall know them by their Fruits · Richard Charles 61

164